ZWINGLI

ZWINGLI

An Introduction to his Thought

W. P. STEPHENS

CLARENDON PRESS · OXFORD
1992

Oxford University Press, Walton Street, Oxford OX2 6DP
Oxford New York Toronto
Delhi Bombay Calcutta Madras Karachi
Petaling Jaya Singapore Hong Kong Tokyo
Nairobi Dar es Salaam Cape Town
Melbourne Auckland
and associated companies in
Berlin Ibadan

Oxford is a trade mark of Oxford University Press

Published in the United States
by Oxford University Press, New York

British Library Cataloguing in Publication Data
(Data available)
ISBN 0–19–826329–5

Library of Congress Cataloging in Publication Data
Stephens, W. P. (W. Peter)
Zwingli: an introduction to his thought/W. P. Stephens.
Includes bibliographical references and index.
1. Zwingli, Ulrich, 1484–1531. I. Title.
BR346.S74 1992
230'.42'092—dc20
ISBN 0–19–826329–5

Typeset by Butler & Tanner Ltd, Frome and London
Printed in Great Britain by
Bookcraft (Bath) Ltd
Midsomer Norton, Avon

To
Kenneth and Florence
Sheelagh, Michael, and Alastair

Preface

MOST people look to Calvin and Geneva as the source and norm of what it is to be Reformed. Indeed the words Reformed and Calvinist are often used interchangeably. Yet central as Calvin's role was in forming the Reformed tradition, both through his ministry and his writings, he was not alone. There were others both before and after him who had a vital role in its formation and development. (To this the monument of the Reformation in Geneva bears witness.) Notable among them is Huldrych Zwingli.

Geneva pledged itself on Sunday 21 May 1536 to live by the Word of God, two months before Calvin arrived in Geneva. It was, however, twenty years earlier that Zwingli turned to Christ and scripture, the moment that marked the first and fundamental step on his path as a reformer. At the end of 1518 he began his ministry in Zurich, and through his lead at the first disputation in January 1523 the Reformation was established in Zurich. He had a profound impact not only in Zurich but also in other parts of Switzerland and the cities of southern Germany. A student of the Reformation needs to look to Zwingli and not only to Luther to understand the origin and scope of the Reformation, just as a student of the Reformed tradition needs to look to Zwingli and Zurich and not only to Calvin and Geneva to understand the Reformed tradition.

For those seeking to do this and who read only in English, there is a growing literature. There are several volumes of his works in English, more indeed than in modern German or any other modern language. There are also many studies of his life, both those written in and those translated into English. But there has till now been no comprehensive introduction to his thought. It is hoped that this study will serve both those whose primary interest is in Zwingli's thought and who can grasp the theological issues involved and those whose primary interest is in his life and work but who want to discover what it is that he believed and preached.

Zwingli's thought is set in the context of his life and ministry. At the end in a chapter on Zwingli as a theologian and reformer, some indication is given of what is central in his thought and his way of working as a reformer. Here—but also in a measure elsewhere—something of Zwingli's relevance for today can be discerned.

I am grateful to Dr Carl Trueman for help with the index.

W.P.S.

Aberdeen
27 February 1991

Contents

Abbreviations

ARG	*Archiv für Reformationsgeschichte* (Berlin, 1903–).
CQR	*Church Quarterly Review* (London, 1875–).
Jackson	S. M. Jackson, *Huldreich Zwingli* (New York, 1901; repr. 1969).
LCC	The Library of Christian Classics (London, 1953–70).
MQR	*Mennonite Quarterly Review* (Goshen, Ind., 1927–).
S	M. Schuler and J. Schulthess, *Huldreich Zwingli's Werke* (Zurich, 1828–42).
Selected Works	S. M. Jackson, *The Selected Works of Huldreich Zwingli* (Philadelphia, 1901; repr., 1972).
SJT	*Scottish Journal of Theology* (Edinburgh, 1948–).
WA	*D. Martin Luthers Werke*, Kritische Gesamtausgabe (Weimar, 1883–).
Works i	S. M. Jackson, *The Latin Works and the Correspondence of Huldreich Zwingli*, i. *1510–1522* (New York, 1912; repr. as *Ulrich Zwingli Early Writings*, Durham, NC, 1987).
Works ii	W. J. Hinke, *The Latin Works of Huldreich Zwingli*, ii (Philadelphia, 1922; repr. as *Zwingli on Providence and Other Essays*, Durham, NC, 1983).
Works iii	C. N. Heller, *The Latin Works of Huldreich Zwingli*, iii (Philadelphia, 1929; repr. as *Commentary on True and False Religion*, Durham, NC, 1981).
Writings i	E. J. Furcha, *Selected Writings of Huldrych*

	Zwingli, i. *The Defense of the Reformed Faith* (Allison Park, Pa., 1985).
Writings ii	H. W. Pipkin, *Selected Writings of Huldrych Zwingli*, ii. *In Search of True Religion: Reformation, Pastoral and Eucharistic Writings* (Allison Park, Pa., 1985).
Z	*Huldreich Zwinglis Sämtliche Werke* (Berlin, Leipzig, Zurich, 1905–).
ZWA	*Zwingliana: Beiträge zur Geschichte Zwinglis, der Reformation, und des Protesttestantismus in der Schweiz* (Zurich, 1897–).

Dates from Zwingli's Life and Ministry

1484	Born in Wildhaus (Toggenburg) (1 January)
1489–98	At school in Weesen, Basle, Berne
1498–1506	At university in Vienna and Basle
1506	Priest at Glarus
1513	Accompanied Glarus troops to Novarra
1515	Accompanied Glarus troops to Marignano
1516	Met Erasmus in Basle
	Priest in Einsiedeln
1519	People's Priest in Zurich—at the Great Minster (Grossmünster)
	Ill with the plague
1522	A group broke the Lenten fast
	Zwingli's first reformation writings
	Disputation with friars (21 July)
1523	First Zurich Disputation (29 January)
	Second Zurich Disputation (26–8 October)
1524	Disputation with canons (13–14 January)
	Removal of pictures and statues from Zurich churches
1525	First rebaptisms (by the anabaptists) (21 January)
	The Lord's Supper replaced the Mass (Holy Week)
	Marriage laws (10 May)
	The Prophecy began (19 June)
1526	Disputation in Baden (19 May–9 June)
1527	Alliance with Constance
1528	Alliance with Berne and St Gallen
	Berne Disputation (6–26 January)
1529	Alliance with Basle, Schaffhausen, Biel, and Mühlhausen
	Alliance of Five Cantons with Ferdinand I (22 April)

	First Kappel Peace Treaty (26 June)
	Marburg Colloquy (1–4 October)
1530	Alliance with Hesse
1531	Zwingli's death at Kappel (11 October)

Introduction

ALL figures in the past suffer from their interpreters, who too often see them as the embodiment or antithesis of their own position. Zwingli is no exception in this. He has in turn been welcomed as the liberal among the reformers or repudiated as the rationalist among them. He has been portrayed as the heroic Swiss patriot dying on the field of battle or dismissed as the preacher turned politician who took the sword and deservedly perished by it.

Zwingli has suffered also from historians who see the Reformation in terms of Luther and who measure every other reformer by him. They see Zwingli in terms of Luther, regarding him as a variant of Luther or, especially if they are Lutheran, as a deviant from him.

There is no final picture of Zwingli and his thought, even though some pictures have undoubtedly had their day. All presentations of Zwingli's thought are inevitably coloured by their authors' standpoint or starting-point and by the selection they make of Zwingli's works.

Thus, to take but one example, a writer's standpoint on the question of how and when Zwingli became a reformer will colour his presentation of Zwingli's thought. For some, Zwingli had essentially Erasmian views of reform until he read Luther. It was through Luther that he became a reformer. After that he was to be understood—as he was by Köhler—as a combination of Luther and Erasmus, a merging of the two streams of Christianity and classical antiquity, or—as he was by others—as a Lutheran reformer who became less Lutheran in the course of the 1520s.

For others, however, Zwingli became a reformer independently of Luther, influenced especially by Erasmus and Augustine, but influenced also by a range of factors and people in the way he developed as a reformer and theologian. In this approach Zwingli's relation to Luther is important but not all important. It should, moreover, not be allowed to dominate the presentation of Zwingli's thought, as that distorts Zwingli's thought which should be presented in its own terms and in its own accents. That is the conviction which underlies this study.

Presentations of Zwingli have equally been coloured by the selection made of his writings as well as by the standpoint of the author. Thus those who emphasize Zwingli's treatise *The Providence of God* get a much more philosophical view of his theology than those who draw on any other of his writings. Those who present his view of the sacraments chiefly from the years 1524 and 1525 get a much more symbolic view (see Glossary) of the sacraments than those who choose the years 1530 and 1531.

In this introduction to Zwingli I endeavour to unfold Zwingli's thought historically. Writings are examined from every period of his life, beginning with his earlier ones where that helps to show development in his thought. The whole range of his writings is drawn on—not only the more systematic ones, but also the letters, commentaries, tracts, and treatises. The factors which shaped his thought, both before and after his move to Zurich, are noted.

Through the centuries there have been many different presentations of Zwingli. Indeed whole books have been written on the changing picture of Zwingli in both Protestant and Roman Catholic writers. There is no space for such a presentation here, though in the course of this study various interpretations will be noted. There are however important areas where the interpretations of recent scholars differ.

First, there is the question of the influences on Zwingli's development, including not only the relative importance of Erasmus, Luther, and Augustine, but also the type of humanist and scholastic thought which he encountered.

Then there is the question of when he emerged as a reformer whether as early as 1516 or not until after his arrival in Zurich, probably as late as 1520 or 1521. This is a theological as well as a historical issue, for it raises the question of how the Reformation is to be defined. Is it to be defined in terms of Luther and the doctrine of justification, and if not is it to be defined ecclesiologically in terms of the break with Rome, or theologically in terms of the authority of scripture, or religiously in terms of the understanding of salvation?

The question of change or development in Zwingli touches particularly on his interpretation of the eucharist, his view of church and state, and his understanding of God. First, did his interpretation of the eucharist change, as Köhler argued, from the medieval view of transubstantiation, to a mystical Erasmian view of Christ's presence, to a purely symbolic view of his presence, to a view of faith-presence? Or is there an evolution or development of his thought, rather than a change, so that it can be said that he always held a broadly symbolic interpretation, with the letter of Hoen simply providing a clue for him to present his symbolic view more satisfactorily? Secondly, did he, as Yoder argued, have a more free-church view of church and state in the early 1520s and then change to a more state-church view? Or did he always have a strong sense of the community as a whole, though perhaps with a somewhat increased emphasis on the role of the council in the second half of the 1520s? Thirdly, did he move from a more biblical or Lutheran view of God and the Christian faith in the early 1520s (in, for example, *An Exposition of the Articles*) to a more philosophical view in the middle and later 1520s (in, for example, *The Providence of God*)? Or is there continuity between these periods, so that a work like *The Providence of God*, if set in the context of his earlier writings, can be seen in a less philosophical light than appears at first sight? Is there in other words a fundamental coherence between Zwingli's various writings, which are fundamentally biblical, but which always reflect the distinctive influences of Erasmus and Augustine?

The relation of church and state in Zwingli raises other questions as well, both concerning Zwingli's political role in the city (which is a matter of continuing discussion among scholars) and concerning the shift that some see to a greater stress on the Old Testament in the later Zwingli, especially in his understanding of the prophet. Zwingli undoubtedly exercised a political role in the city, though he was never, as it was once put, minister and mayor, councillor and clerk, all in one person. He certainly saw the situation of church and society in Zurich as more like that of the Old Testament than that of the New, but he was still expounding the New Testament as well as the Old Testament in the second half of the 1520s.

In all these areas there is debate among Zwingli scholars, as well as in some other matters which will be examined, such as whether Zwingli was a Nestorian in his understanding of Christ, and a spiritualist in his understanding of the Spirit.

This introduction to Zwingli's thought opens with a brief chapter on Zurich and the Swiss confederation which were the context of Zwingli's life and work. There follows a longer biographical chapter in which his thought is set in the context of his life and work and in the context of his development in the time both before and after he became a reformer. It helps to show that his thought is not divorced from his life and work, but is his response both to the word of God on the one hand and to the events and people he was dealing with on the other. In some subjects such as baptism, his theology was developed only because he faced challenges to which he had to respond and without which it is likely that he would have written little or nothing on certain subjects.

The central concerns in Zwingli's theology are expounded in the remaining chapters. The first deals with the Bible because that is the basis of Zwingli's reforming ministry and his theology. Then come the main subjects which he treats directly and indirectly in his works. They are referred to directly in commentaries and treatises and in his more systematic and confessional works. But in some cases they are also referred to by Zwingli indirectly as doctrines which underlie and shape other parts of his teaching. Thus the sovereignty of God is so fundamental an element in Zwingli's thought that it affects all aspects of his theology. It is a presupposition of much of what he wrote. (You could almost say that it is the key in which his theology is composed.) Again the way he understands Christ and the Spirit is a major factor in what he has to say, for example, about word and sacrament. These different subjects are related and cannot be divorced from each other, though they are necessarily treated separately.

The final chapter points to some of the characteristic notes in Zwingli's work as a reformer and some of the emphases in his thought.

A study of Zwingli raises the question of the impact of Zwingli not only in his life but also after his death. Relatively little has been written on this, although G. W. Locher has written on Zwingli's influence in England and Scotland in the sixteenth century.

Zwingli's influence after his death was direct and indirect. It was made directly through his writings and indirectly through Bullinger and others who continued his work and reflected or developed his theology. The impact is clearest in two areas: the relation of church and state and the understanding of the sacraments, especially the eucharist.

In Zwingli's writings and in his work in Zurich there is a sense of church and society as one, with the government or council involved in the ordering of the life of the church. This had an impact in parts of Switzerland and beyond. It was distinct from the other Reformed tradition in, for example, Calvin and Geneva, which sought independence from government in the ordering of the church's life and in particular in the matter of discipline.

Zwingli's view of the sacraments and in particular of the eucharist was more influential both then and now. It was maintained though somewhat modified by Bullinger in the Zurich Agreement (*Consensus Tigurinus*) which united Zurich and Geneva in 1549. Zwingli's view made a strong impression on the English Reformation, especially through some of the continental exiles, and is manifest in much popular Protestant thought today. The question of whether Cranmer was a Zwinglian is still debated.

Some elements in his theology were developed by others. Bullinger in particular developed Zwingli's theology of the covenant, which was to be so important in later Reformed teaching. Like Zwingli in his doctrine of predestination, Bullinger laid the stress on election, so that both sides appealed to him in later controversy over election and reprobation. Moreover some of the ways in which Reformed theology differs from Lutheran theology show its kinship with Zwingli, especially in the understanding of gospel and law (rather than law and gospel) and in some of the emphases in the understanding of God and the relation of the divine and human natures in Christ.

Of his reformation practices the most influential was the prophecy. Its impact can be seen in the development of prophesyings in the English Reformation. His practice of expounding whole books of the Bible rather than the appointed readings for the day is still used in some churches today.

I

Zurich and the Confederation

NO one can be isolated from the time and place in which he lives and works—and Zwingli can certainly not be isolated from Switzerland at the end of the fifteenth and the beginning of the sixteenth century. In this chapter and the next Zwingli's work and thought will be set in the immediate context of his life and the wider context of the city and the confederation in which he ministered.

The Swiss Confederation

The Swiss confederation in which Zwingli lived had a complex history. In 1291 Uri, Schwyz, and Unterwalden entered into an alliance which marked the beginning of the confederation. They were joined by Lucerne in 1332, Zurich in 1352, and Glarus, Zug, and Berne, bringing the number to eight by 1353. Others joined later (Fribourg and Solothurn in 1481, Basle and Schaffhausen in 1501, and finally Appenzell in 1513) making a total of thirteen. Despite this long development Swiss independence of the Holy Roman Empire was probably not formally recognized until 1648. However it was effective from the Peace of Basle in 1499.

Besides these thirteen states (Orte or Stände) which were later called cantons, there were other places in a variety of relationships with them. These included seven allies or affiliated states (Zugewandten) and a number of mandated territories (Gemeine Herrschaften). Among the former were the Valais and the Grisons, St Gallen, the Abbey of St Gallen, Mühlhausen, and Biel.

The states were very different in nature and size. Some were relatively small rural communities, such as the three original states, while others were flourishing city-states, such as Basle, Berne, and Zurich. However regardless of size they were constitutionally equal and independent. Their representatives met in a federal diet, but the diet did not have political or economic powers. Decisions were taken by the separate states. This independence of the various states was an important factor both in the spread of the Reformation and in the opposition to it. It was also a factor in the mandated territories where the decision was that of the majority of the ruling states.

The Swiss were notable at this time for their military prowess. They had been victorious in a number of crucial battles in their first formative century: Morgarten (1315), Sempach (1386), and Näfels (1388). Their success in war continued and led to their being regarded as valuable soldiers in the armies of France, Austria, and other powers, including the papacy. Substantial annual sums or pensions were paid to leading Swiss figures in order to enlist mercenaries. A catastrophic defeat by the French at Marignano in 1515, when the Swiss had switched sides to the pope, led to renewed support for the French, except in Zurich. Zwingli's hostility to the French alliance was to be a factor working against him in Glarus, and working with him in his move to Zurich.

Zwingli's reforming ministry was primarily in Zurich, but his sense of being Swiss and not just a Zuricher or Toggenburger meant that he had his eye on winning the whole confederation to the gospel of Christ. Initially however he had to win a hearing for it in Zurich and then build on the response to it there. The difficulties and opportunities he faced in this were related in part to the civil and religious character of the city and its surrounding territory.

Zurich

Zurich was a city of 5,000–6,000 (the exact figure is a matter of debate) with a population of some 50,000 in the whole state. The city had a long history. There was a settlement there in Roman times, but it was the establishing of a community of Benedictine nuns in 853 which led to the development of the city. By 1218 it had become a full imperial city. In 1336 the craftsmen, led by Rudolf Brun, turned it into a guild city. It was then organized in thirteen guilds (later there were to be twelve), with Brun as mayor. In 1351 it entered into an alliance with the three original Swiss states (Uri, Schwyz, and Unterwalden) and Lucerne which had already joined them. Through the succeeding centuries it grew in size and importance.

The city was governed by two councils. The Great Council had 162 members. They were drawn from the twelve craft guilds (twelve from each) together with eighteen from the constables, a body made up of nobles, property owners, and merchants. The Small Council which was in effect a cabinet or executive body had fifty members. Strictly speaking there were two such councils, with twenty-five members, headed by a mayor, governing for six months each. Eventually, however, they met together. There were also representatives in the Small Council of the guilds and constables. As there could be changes in the mayor and membership every six months, there was a regular possibility of changing policy. (Another important factor in the development of the Reformation was the shift of power in the first part of the sixteenth century from the constables to the guilds.) The Great and Small Councils together made up the Council of the Two Hundred (strictly speaking 212 members). It was concerned with matters such as alliances, major appointments, peace, and war.

There were at different times commissions to advise on particular matters. These bodies exercised considerable influence, and it was in part through his advice to them or participation in them that Zwingli made his impact on the council. His role was, however, essentially indirect, for he was never himself a member of the council.

The Church in Zurich

Switzerland was not a coherent whole in church government. There was no archbishop and the dioceses overlapped Switzerland and the neighbouring countries of France, Germany, and Italy. Zurich itself was in the large diocese of Constance, whose bishop, Hugo von Hohenlandberg, had in his diocese some 1,800 parishes and over 15,000 priests. There were about 500 priests in the city-state and some 200 in the city of Zurich.

The low moral standards of the priests are evident in a letter of Bishop Hugo in May 1516. He spoke of a number of their failings, including concubinage. The council had, indeed, already complained about concubinage both to the bishop and the pope.

Among the clergy the vow of celibacy was widely broken, and it seems that in one year 1,500 children were born to priests in the diocese. (Priests had to pay four or five gulden to the bishop for such offences.) However concubinage did not cause the surprise or offence that it would today, and there were priests who lived acceptably in their parishes with a wife and children. A notable example in Switzerland was in Bremgarten, where the father of Heinrich Bullinger, Zwingli's successor in Zurich, had been priest. The widespread practice of concubinage helps to explain the relative ease with which people accepted the marriage of the reformers. It is also one reason why the reformers wrestled with the biblical material bearing on the case for the freedom of priests to marry.

The council exercised a growing role in church affairs, including the right to appoint to posts in the Great Minster and the Minster of our Lady. (It appointed Zwingli to the Great Minster in 1518.) The Great Minster (Grossmünster) and the Minster of our Lady (Fraumünster) were founded in the ninth century. The latter was a monastery for Benedictine nuns. The first abbess, Hildegard, was the daughter of King Lewis the German, who founded and endowed it. The abbess had once exercised great power, including the right to mint coins and collect tolls on goods. By the time of the Reformation the monastery had considerably diminished numbers and its powers had mostly passed to the city. The last abbess transferred it to the city in November 1524. Besides the two minsters there were five other places of pilgrimage in Zurich: St Peter's Church, the cloisters of the Dominicans, Franciscans, and Augustinian Hermits, and the Water Church (Wasserkirche). The Dominicans and Franciscans came to the city in the first half of the thirteenth century, and the Augustinians in the second half. There were also communities of Dominican nuns.

It is in this republican setting, with power exercised by a council rather than by a single ruler, that Zwingli lived and worked. The changing balance of power in the various groups (both civil and religious) helps to account for the kind of reformer Zwingli became and the kind of reformation he introduced.

2

Zwingli's Life and Ministry

NOT two months separated the birth of Martin Luther in 1483 from that of Huldrych Zwingli on 1 January 1484. Born at Wildhaus, high up in the Toggenburg, he was the son of a farmer, who was the Ammann (or magistrate) of the community. He went as a young boy to his uncle Bartholomew, a priest in Wesen, to begin his education. He showed promise there and at the age of 10 he was sent to the school of Gregory Bünzli in Basle to learn Latin. Four years later he moved to Henry Wölflin's school in Berne, where—among other things—he studied Latin literature. Then in 1498, at the age of 14, he went to the university of Vienna, where the great humanist Conrad Celtis taught. At 18 he matriculated in the university of Basle, where Thomas Wyttenbach was one of his teachers. Among his fellow students were Leo Jud and Conrad Pellican, later to be colleagues in Zurich. He graduated there as Bachelor of Arts in 1504 and as Master of Arts in 1506. Then, at the age of 22, while he was still a layman, he was called to be priest at Glarus.

He was ordained in Constance in September 1506, several weeks before reaching the canonical age for ordination. He preached his first sermon at Rapperswil and then celebrated his first mass in Wildhaus on St Michael's and All Angels. He was a priest in Glarus for a decade. It was a period in which, alongside his duties as a priest, he learned Greek and developed his humanist studies. It was not till the end of that time that Zwingli began to emerge as a reformer, but in those ten years and in the years before we see three of the important influences on his later work as a reformer: patriotism, scholasticism, and humanism.

Patriotism, Scholasticism, Humanism

Zwingli was intensely patriotic. He was a patriot all his days. In 1526 he recalled that from his boyhood, he had resisted any who slandered or abused the Swiss, even putting himself in danger (Z V 250. 6–11).[1] It is a testimony to his patriotism that the earliest writing of his that we have, written in 1510 when he was 26, is a patriotic poem called *The Ox*. The poem is an attack—in the form of an allegory—on the use of Swiss mercenaries to fight for foreign powers. At that stage, in his loyalty to the papacy, he made an exception of fighting for the pope, but soon he allowed no exceptions whatsoever. However his support for the papacy led to his receiving an annual pension of fifty gulden until he surrendered it in 1520.

His opposition to mercenary service was deepened by his firsthand experience of war as a chaplain in 1513 and 1515, and perhaps in 1512 as well. In September 1515 he witnessed the disastrous battle of Marignano, in which thousands of Swiss soldiers died, fighting as mercenaries against the French. These experiences made him even more aware of the devastation of war and the profound moral and social cost that it brought to his people. In a second poem, *The Labyrinth*, he again used an allegory to attack the mercenary system. This time however the patriotism was explicitly religious. 'In us there is no love of God.... Whoever commits crime and murder is considered a bold man. Did Christ teach us that? ... Tell me what have we of Christians more than the name?' (Z I 60.) His attacks on the mercenary system and in particular on the alliance with the French, which was favoured in Glarus, provoked opposition to him in Glarus, and lay behind his moving from there to Einsiedeln in 1516.

If his patriotism dates from his boyhood, the influence of scholasticism stems from his time at university. At Basle he was influenced by Thomas Wyttenbach, an exponent of the the old way (*via antiqua*), with the writings of Thomas Aquinas, Peter Lombard, and Duns Scotus. (That contrasts with Luther who

[1] For an explanation of references in the text, see the sections on 'Zwingli's Works' and 'Zwingli's Works in English' in the Bibliography.

was influenced by the modern way (*via moderna*), though Zwingli almost certainly met both traditions in Basle.) In Zwingli's library there is evidence of his reading Aquinas and Duns Scotus, and in a letter of 1511 he is spoken of as being an Aristotelian. There may be signs of Scotist influence in his theology in the emphasis on the will of God, in the contrast between the creator and the creature, in the stress on the eucharist as a commemoration of Christ's sacrifice, and perhaps in his christology as well. However scholars vary in their assessment of Zwingli, with Locher pointing to Thomism and the old way (*via antiqua*) and Pollet, a Dominican, pointing to Occamism and the modern way (*via moderna*). Yet, although Zwingli rejected scholastic theology, he did not escape its influence. Moreover he made use later of its methods and distinctions in debate, not least in the debate on the eucharist.

Humanism probably influenced Zwingli at school and at university. Some argue particularly for the influence of Celtis in Vienna, although little can be said about this with certainty. During his time at Glarus (1506–16), however, he emerged as a humanist. He read widely and eagerly. His love of classical antiquity can be seen in the library which he built up and which he later took with him from Glarus to Einsiedeln, with its annotated copies of Aristotle, Cicero, Demosthenes, Homer, Juvenal, Livy, Pliny, and Plutarch. His correspondence at this time with Beatus Rhenanus, Glarean, and Conrad Pellican testifies, as Farner points out, to a humanist scholar rather than to a priest or theologian.[2]

A decisive change occurred when he met Erasmus in 1515 or 1516. Erasmus, the prince of the humanists, was a classical scholar, as well as a biblical and patristic scholar. His humanist concern for the sources led not only to the study of the language and literature of Greece and Rome, but also to that of the New Testament and the fathers. He published an edition of the Greek New Testament and an elegant Latin translation of the New Testament, as well as notable editions of the fathers. He worked for a rebirth of Christianity.

[2] O. Farner, *Huldrych Zwingli* (Zurich, 1946), ii. 109.

It was the impact of Erasmus that pointed Zwingli in a new way to Christ and to the scriptures. For Zwingli Erasmus had freed the scriptures from scholasticism, and under his influence Zwingli became a theologian not in a scholastic but in a humanist sense. He turned to the sources, in particular the Greek New Testament; he studied the fathers; he learned the historical, critical approach to the text. It is now the fathers rather than the schoolmen who engaged Zwingli, and they are widely represented in his library which came to include editions of Ambrose, Athanasius, Augustine, Basil, Chrysostom, Cyprian, Eusebius, Jerome, and Origen, and various works of Cyril, Gregory of Nazianzus, Gregory of Nyssa, Hilary of Poitiers, Irenaeus, John of Damascus, and Lactantius.

The first fruit of Erasmus's influence can be seen in *The Labyrinth* which has a religious element missing from *The Ox* three years earlier. The long-term fruit was in a reformation theology that was both biblical and centred in Christ. There are many points of contact between Erasmus and Zwingli. There were shared assumptions—in particular a stress on God as Spirit and a Platonist view of man as body and soul. There were common emphases—in particular the emphasis on an inward rather than an outward piety. There were similar concerns—in particular a delight in the literature and philosophy of Greece and Rome. But there were differences as well, notably but not only in their understanding of the sovereign grace of God and the freedom of the will. The differences can be seen later in Erasmus's criticism of Zwingli's *Archeteles* in 1522, and Zwingli's attack on the freedom of the will in *A Commentary* in 1525. However—unlike Luther—he could still refer positively to Erasmus.

The Early Years in Zurich

From 1516 till 1518, Zwingli ministered in Einsiedeln, a great centre of pilgrimage and famous for its Marian shrine. He continued with the diverse work of a priest: celebrating the sacraments of the church, involved in pilgrimages and in indulgences, exercising pastoral care. He also continued to make a name for himself as a preacher. Then on 28 October 1518 Oswald Myconius wrote to say that there was a vacancy at the Great Minster in Zurich and that he longed to see Zwingli there.

On 3 December however he wrote again to say that various objections had been raised against Zwingli, including one which he could not answer: that he had wronged the daughter of a prominent citizen of Einsiedeln. Zwingli's reply was found in the nineteenth century by the Zwingli scholar, Johannes Schulthess. Oscar Farner records that Schulthess showed it to his pupil Alexander Schweizer and then placed it in the flame of a candle to burn it. However he withdrew it in time, uttering the defiant words, 'Protestantism is the truth in all circumstances.'[3] This letter of Zwingli was one in which he admitted that he had—despite great efforts—been unchaste, but that his unchastity was now a thing of the past. His letter satisfied the chapter, and he was elected on 11 December by seventeen votes to seven. (Zwingli's unchastity was far from exceptional in the sixteenth century, and an alternative candidate was said to have fathered six children.)

Zwingli's ministry in Zurich began on 1 January 1519, his 35th birthday. As he had promised in his acceptance, he began the following day to preach on St Matthew—but in a new way. He preached consecutively through the gospel, as indeed some of the fathers had done, and not on the passage for the day. (Z VII 106.3–4.) (He was later to claim that his preaching before he came to Zurich had been on the basis of scripture and not on the basis of the fathers (Z II 144.32–145.8).) After expounding St Matthew and the Acts he turned to 1 Timothy, Galatians, 2 Timothy, 1 and 2 Peter, and Hebrews, choosing the books which would speak to the people's need at the time (Z I 133.2–5; 284.39–285.25). He wrote of the role of his preaching in the words: 'This is the seed I have sown, Matthew, Luke, Paul and Peter have watered it and God has given it splendid increase, but this I will not trumpet forth, lest I seem to be canvassing my own glory and not Christ's.' (Z I 285.25–8; *Works* i. 239.) By the end of 1519 Zwingli spoke of 'two thousand

[3] Farner, *Huldrych Zwingli*, ii. 298–9.

rational souls, who now feeding on spiritual milk, will soon take solid food' (Z VII 245.15–16), although the same letter refers to the opposition he was facing.

The first year in Zurich was an eventful one. Between August 1519 and February 1520 almost a quarter of the inhabitants of Zurich died of the plague. Zwingli, who was out of Zurich, returned to his pastoral duties in the city. In September he was himself taken ill and came close to death. It was some time after this that he wrote a poem, *The Plague Song*, which manifests his sense of God's sovereignty and his submission to God's will.

In July 1519 Luther engaged in the Leipzig disputation, at which he challenged the divine right of the papacy. This was a decisive experience for Zwingli, who hailed Luther as a new Elijah, and in 1520 Zwingli took the symbolically important step of renouncing the papal pension which he had enjoyed since his time in Glarus. (In 1523 Zwingli wrote that he had renounced it in 1517, but that it was still paid until his written renunciation in 1520 (Z II 314.2–21).) Some see this step as the evidence that he had come to a reformation faith.

The year 1520 was marked by an important decision of the city council, as it determined that preaching should be in accordance with scripture. This was no doubt a victory for Zwingli whose preaching was scriptural. It is on the basis of scripture that he attacked a number of beliefs and practices of the medieval church, such as indulgences, tithes, and the invocation of the saints—attacks which in their turn provoked opposition to him. On issues such as these he drew support from Luther's works and encouraged the sale of Luther's books as part of his own battle for reform in the church. Luther features constantly in his correspondence at this time, but Zwingli did not seem to see in him anything more than a support for positions which he already held. Luther's distinctively reformation concerns (such as the theology of the cross and justification by faith) are certainly not explicit in Zwingli's references to him. Along with the reading of Luther, there is the study of Augustine's tractates on John, and the study of John and Paul, which were to be so important in the maturing of his theology.

Yet Zwingli remains in many ways a humanist in his concerns.

In particular his correspondence testifies to the strong literary and political interests of Swiss humanism. Some would see a decisive change from the reforming humanist to the reformer in 1520, and point especially to Zwingli's letter to Myconius on 24 July. The letter certainly shows how much opposition Zwingli faced in his ministry in Zurich, although at that time he still had good relations with the hierarchy. In it he wrote that he intended to urge the papal legate to warn the pope not to excommunicate Luther. He is, however, himself prepared for the possibility of excommunication. 'I entreat Christ for this one thing, that he grant me to bear all things manfully and that, as a potter's vessel, he break or strengthen me, as it pleases him.' (Z VII 344.15–17.) The letter is dated significantly on the eve of the feast of James, the son of Zebedee, who was the first of the apostles to be a martyr.

In March 1522 there was a decisive public step when Christoph Froschauer, the famous Zurich printer, and others ate meat in Lent—on the ground that an unusually heavy amount of work demanded it. Zwingli did not himself break the Lenten fast with them, but he preached a sermon in support of them, arguing for Christian liberty. It is from this sermon—some would say from a poem, *The Mill*—that most scholars see a clearly evangelical note in Zwingli's writings. (However few of Zwingli's writings have survived from before this—only three poems, some letters, and an account of a battle—which makes judgement in this matter difficult.) For Zwingli, however, this was not a new departure in his ministry, for when he published the sermon, he began by stating that the people had been responding eagerly to the gospel he had been preaching for over three years.

In a work published in May the issue he raised was not an individual one, as it had been with the Lenten fast, but a national one: the question of Swiss mercenaries. Of all the dangers which he saw, the gravest was not the moral corruption or political subjugation to which the mercenary system led, but the fact that it placed the whole people under God's wrath. *A Solemn Exhortation* was addressed to Schwyz, the state in which Zwingli had worked while a priest in Einsiedeln. It shows that Zwingli's challenge was to the whole life of the people and not just its religious life, and to civil leaders and not just ecclesiastical ones. This concern with the total life of society was characteristic of the whole of Zwingli's reforming ministry.

In July 1522 there was an appeal for clerical marriage, as well as debates with Francis Lambert, a Franciscan, on the intercession of the saints, and with members of the religious orders in Zurich on the authority of scripture. Running through his preaching and writing in 1522 was the appeal to scripture against all human teaching, and hence a challenge to the authority of the church. This issue came to a head in the first disputation in January 1523 where judgement was to be made on the basis of scripture.

Zwingli saw the disputation, to which over 600 people came, as an opportunity to expound and defend the faith—and to do so in German and not, as in an academic disputation, in Latin. (Disputations were to become an important means of spreading and establishing the Reformation in Switzerland and southern Germany.) He presented sixty-seven articles which embodied what he had been preaching. They expressed two fundamental contrasts: between the authority of scripture and the authority of the church and between seeking salvation through Christ and seeking it through anyone or anything else. The central place of Christ is unmistakable, and the first twenty-three articles are all related specifically to Christ. However Zwingli's opponent, John Faber, vicar general of Constance, raised the question of authority, shrewdly asking whether it was not the council that was the judge between them. Zwingli, however, insisted that the judge was scripture. At the end of the debate the council, which had summoned the disputation because of the dissension in Zurich, gave its judgement that Zwingli's preaching was scriptural and that everyone should preach in accordance with scripture.

In July 1523 Zwingli published *An Exposition of the Articles*. It is the most substantial treatment of his theology in German and manifests most of his distinctive emphases. It is characteristic of him that his sixty-seven articles cover a whole programme of reform, social and political, as well as ecclesiastical and personal. They can be contrasted with Luther's ninety-five theses which deal with the single issue of indulgences. With the articles and their exposition it can be said that the inauguration of the Reformation in Zurich was complete.

Becoming a Reformer

The question of when Zwingli became a reformer is one of the most disputed and fascinating questions in Zwingli study. Scholars are divided about when it happened and what caused it to happen. Some place it as early as 1516, others as late as 1521. Some see the decisive influence in Erasmus, others in Luther or Augustine.

The question is complicated by the evidence available to us. The only contemporary evidence is in the marginal notes Zwingli made in his books. There is naturally a problem in dating marginal notes. However a century ago Usteri discovered two clues for dating them: the colour of the ink and the writing of the letter d. He argued that Zwingli wrote d with its tail below the line up to July 1519 and above it from then. This is the time of the Leipzig disputation which made a strong impact on Zwingli. The change in the colour of the ink dates from the time of his contact with Erasmus. However there are still problems in dating the notes, and there is the further problem that they show what Zwingli noted in others or from others, and not necessarily what he learnt from them.

Zwingli's own view is clear. He dated his preaching of the gospel from the time when he turned to Christ and scripture, probably in 1516. Yet, as we study his writings, that seems the decisive moment rather than the final one. It is not till 1522 that Zwingli's writings manifest a full sense of the grace of God in Jesus Christ. What began in 1516 did not fully mature till several years later.

Zwingli, however, always pointed to the earlier date. There are several occasions in the 1520s when he referred to the time that he had begun to preach the gospel, and the general picture that emerges is clear and coherent, even if the year is not clear. He asserted his independence of Luther and invoked God as witness that he had learned the gospel from John, Augustine's tractates on John, and Paul's epistles. He referred to Thomas Wyttenbach's disputation in Basle, probably in 1515, which showed indulgences to be a deceit, and to the poem of Erasmus, from which he derived his faith that no one except Christ can mediate between God and us. He took up the poem's lament that people do not seek all their good in Christ, the fount of all good. For Zwingli the fundamental difference between himself and his opponents was between trusting in Christ and his atoning death and trusting in the creature. Therefore, he naturally regarded the making of that discovery as the fundamental turning-point in his life. This also means that, like Bucer and unlike Luther, he did not see a fundamental contrast between Erasmus and the Reformation.

Zwingli's preaching of the gospel embraced both his turning to Christ and his turning to scripture. In *The Clarity and Certainty of the Word of God* in 1522 he spoke of having begun seven or eight years before to rely wholly on scripture, learning God's teaching from his own plain word, and seeking understanding from God rather than from commentaries and expositors. In the same year there is reference in *Archeteles* to trusting God's word alone for salvation.

It is noteworthy that Zwingli saw a continuity not only between his understanding of scripture and the gospel in 1522 and 1523 (when undoubtedly there is a reformation understanding of them) and what he held in his early years in Zurich, but also between that and what he held in Einsiedeln or at the end of his time in Glarus (Z I 88.10–89 2; II 14.11–14), which is a period in which most scholars see him as an Erasmian rather than as a reformer. Zwingli's sense of continuity in his ministry fits the way in which Bucer—twenty years later—saw the continuity between Erasmus and Luther and wrote of Erasmus as showing that salvation comes from faith in Christ and not from ceremonies. Zwingli regarded both Erasmus and Luther as raised up by God, and he recognized, beside scripture, both their part and that of the fathers in learning what true religion is.

The decisive role of Erasmus cannot be doubted—but what

of Luther and Augustine? Zwingli certainly denied that he learnt the gospel from Luther, and claimed to have begun preaching it two years before people in his area had heard of Luther. There is naturally the suspicion that Zwingli wanted to assert his independence of Luther, in part at least because of the danger of being identified with a heretic. However there are good reasons for accepting his assertion that he was independent, although some scholars still make a case for Zwingli's dependence. The research of Rich has shown that when Zwingli read Luther, he seemed to find in Luther confirmation of views he already held and to see Luther as supporting what we may describe as a reforming rather than a reformation position. For Zwingli what was decisive in Luther was his deed rather than his words—the fact that at the Leipzig disputation he had had the courage to act against the pope, like a David against Goliath.

The exact role of Augustine is also difficult to determine. It is bound up with the dating of Zwingli's marginal notes. It seems that Zwingli studied Augustine in Glarus and Einsiedeln as well as in Zurich, and Augustine was certainly a stimulus in the deepening of Zwingli's grasp of scripture and the gospel, as he himself stated. Moreover important elements and emphases in Zwingli's theology can be found in the marginal notes on Augustine. But besides the question of their date there is the question whether Augustine led to a further study of the Bible or whether the study of the Bible led to a study of Augustine and other fathers in order to understand the Bible better. The similarities between Augustine and Zwingli are, however, wide and deep. They can be found not only in their understanding of the sovereignty and righteousness of God, but also in their understanding of scripture and the sacraments, as well as in the Platonist cast of their theology.

There are probably many factors that lie behind the change that took place in 1515–16: not only matters such as the learning of Greek, the disputation of Wyttenbach, the reading of Erasmus's poem, the meeting with Erasmus and the intensive study of his works, and the copying out of Paul's letters in Greek, but also perhaps experiences such as the disastrous defeat of the Swiss which he witnessed at Marignano in September 1515, and his own sexual lapse when a priest in Einsiedeln. Yet important as the change in 1515–16 was, there is no doubt that Zwingli came to a profounder grasp of the gospel and scripture in his first years in Zurich. Various experiences contributed to this: his study of John, Augustine, and Paul (whenever this is dated); the example of Luther in Leipzig in 1519; his suffering from the plague in the same year and his later reflection on this in a poem; the apparent failure of his successful ministry in Zurich to which a letter of 24 July 1520 testifies; and an undated occasion when—in wrestling with the words 'Forgive us our trespasses, as we forgive those that trespass against us'—he came to see and accept his utter dependence on God's grace.

Yet whatever the influence of these various experiences, none should exclude the formative role of scripture itself. In it he met the living word of God and sensed God's overwhelming grace. Alongside scripture, however, we cannot ignore the role of two of its interpreters: Erasmus and Augustine.

Conservative and Radical Opponents

Zwingli found himself with opponents on both sides—those resisting reformation and those wanting a reformation which was more radical than his. The radicals differed not only in their interpretation of the Bible, with their emphasis on the New Testament, but also in their understanding of the church and the Christian life. They took issue with him on tithes and the paying of interest, and later on images, oaths, baptism, and the eucharist. They disagreed with Zwingli on both the content of the reformation and its pace.

The radicals were at first closely identified with Zwingli—some had broken the Lenten fast in 1522. In the early days Zwingli often met with them. In the summer of 1522 they were joined by Felix Manz and Conrad Grebel, the son of a city councillor. The following year, on 22 June, a delegation from several parishes met the council and raised among other things the question of tithes. Two days later Zwingli preached a sermon, which was expanded into a treatise, *Divine and Human Righteousness*. In it he made the distinction between divine and human righteousness. He argued for respecting property and paying interest and tithes while the government required them, although he criticized them in terms of divine righteousness.

Later in the summer Zwingli was criticized by the radicals for not being biblical enough in his proposals about the mass. For example, he did not reject eucharistic vestments, and for the sake of the weak he allowed the sign of the cross. (In earlier controversy with his Catholic opponents on fasting, he had argued that where there was no prohibition in scripture, then God had left the issue free.) Zwingli regarded his opponents as biblicist. By contrast with them he regarded matters such as the time at which the eucharist was to be celebrated and the question whether the bread should be leavened or unleavened, as ones which the church was free to decide. Moreover he judged that the radicals' concern for immediate action in reform would alienate many people and lead to uproar.

By October, however, after the denunciation and violent destruction of images by the radicals, the council summoned a second disputation to examine images and the mass in the light of scripture. Although the council clearly hoped to make it a federal assembly, the bishops and most of the cantons declined invitations. Nevertheless it was attended by 900 people and its judgement was that the mass and images were unscriptural. Unlike the radicals, however, Zwingli was willing for the council to determine when the changes which had been agreed should take place. The role that Zwingli saw for government (and therefore in Zurich for its governing body, the council) was to become an area of increasing dispute between him and the radicals.

A third disputation was held in January 1524, but this time it was with a small select group. It marked an unsuccessful attempt by the conservatives to undermine the Reformation in Zurich. By June the council agreed to do away with statues and images in response to the word of God, and in a dramatic fortnight they were removed and the churches cleansed. However it was not till the Easter of 1525 that the mass was replaced by the Lord's Supper. Then on Maundy Thursday a table, covered with a clean linen cloth, was set between the choir and nave in the Great Minster. Upon it were the bread on wooden platters and the wine in wooden beakers. The service was in Swiss German, not Latin, with the men and women on opposite sides of the middle aisle. The elements were taken by the appointed ministers through the congregation.

The slowness of reform provoked the radicals. They destroyed images months before the council took action to remove images, and they celebrated their own form of the Lord's Supper in January 1525, several weeks ahead of the reformers. But images and the mass were not the only issues. Soon other matters came into the centre of the conflict with the reformers. There were social and political issues, including obedience to civil authority, which led to Zwingli's writing *Those Who Give Cause for Tumult* in December 1524, as well as the question of infant baptism and eventually rebaptism.

As early as February 1524 a number of people refused to have their children baptized. After an unsuccessful meeting in December between the radicals and Zwingli, along with other ministers, the council summoned the ministers and the radicals to a disputation on 17 January 1525. After it the council insisted that they baptize their infants within eight days, on pain of banishment. However on 21 January a new development took place. On that day opposition to infant baptism led to rebaptism, and Conrad Grebel baptized George Blaurock, who then baptized fifteen others. Further meetings between radicals and reformers were not fruitful, and on 7 March 1526 the council threatened those rebaptizing with death by drowning. On 5 January 1527 Felix Manz was the first to suffer that penalty.

The year 1525 was important in Zurich not only for the first reformed celebration of the Lord's Supper at Easter, but also for the institution of the prophecy (*Prophezei*) in June. The prophecy was a characteristically Zwinglian response to both conservatives and radicals, and expressed his view of the reformed pastor and preacher over against the unreformed priest and the itinerant preacher. At the heart of the prophecy was the study of the Bible in the original languages, Hebrew and Greek. (The understanding of biblical languages was seen as corresponding with the gift of tongues in the New Testament.) For

Zwingli, a preacher versed in the scriptures could keep clear of the errors of those who rely on human teaching, whether they appealed as conservatives did to the teaching of the church or as radicals did to the Spirit. The prophecy was vital for the education of a reformed ministry and manifested the centrality of the word in a reformed church.

In Zwingli's view the whole life of the community was to be brought under the sovereign rule of God. Legislation for the social and political life of the community was as important for him as changes in its liturgical life. In January 1525 the poor law was enacted, and in May marriage laws. This process developed, leading to the great moral mandate in May 1530. Oversight of another kind came with the calling of a synod in 1528 and in succeeding years.

In all these reforms the council was indispensable. Its active role in church affairs was not new, as it had gathered powers to itself in the years before the Reformation, but undoubtedly it sought to extend its powers wherever possible. Zwingli argued for its place in the reformation of the city on theological and practical grounds, but always it was to act in accordance with the word of God, by which everything was to be governed. It was, moreover, not to act on its own, but always with the silent consent of the church. Its representative action was for Zwingli a way in which change could take place peacefully, for an assembly of the whole church might be divisive. However other reformers, such as Bucer, Oecolampadius, and Calvin, sought a more independent role for the church.

The Later Years in Zurich

From the beginning Zwingli's concern was with the whole of the confederation and not just with Zurich. He sought freedom for the preaching of the word in other cantons. For their part the five cantons, Uri, Schwyz, Zug, Lucerne, and Unterwalden, sought to expel Zurich from the federation. The conflict between them expressed itself first in disputation and then in battle.

Zwingli did not take part directly in the disputation with John

Eck at Baden in 1526 because of fears for his safety, although a well-concealed messenger service brought reports to him of the day's debate and took back his comments and suggestions for the next day. The theses advanced by Eck concerned the mass, the intercession of the saints, images, and purgatory, but underlying them all was the question of the authority of scripture. The disputation resulted, as was expected, in a victory for Eck. The defeat was reversed two years later at the disputation in Berne in January 1528, in which Zwingli took part, together with Bucer, Haller, and Oecolampadius. Victory in Berne was a crucial step in the spread of the Reformation in Switzerland, for its dominant role in the west was similar to that of Zurich in the east.

The following year saw disputation give way to battle. In his eagerness to defend the proclamation of the gospel, Zwingli urged an attack on the five cantons. He wrote to Berne, 'Be firm and do not fear war. For that peace which some are so urgently pressing upon us is not peace but war. And the war for which I am so insistent is peace, not war.... Unless this takes place neither the truth of the gospel nor its ministers will be safe among us.' (Z X 147. 2–7.) The war ended almost as soon as it had begun, and a treaty was signed. The reformation cities held that it permitted the preaching of the gospel. However, as the five cantons denied this, there was deadlock.

The same year marked the climax of the conflict between Zwingli and Luther. The main area of disagreement was the eucharist, and there were signs of a different theology in this and in some other matters as early as 1523. At first Zwingli and Luther were not engaged in direct conflict, but in 1527 and 1528 they wrote major works against each other. The need for unity, made more urgent by Catholic opposition to the Reformation, led to the Marburg Colloquy, to which Philip of Hesse invited them in 1529. It produced substantial agreement, although both sides interpreted the Marburg articles somewhat differently. Fourteen of the fifteen articles were agreed and in the fifteenth on the eucharist there was agreement in five points, with the one point of disagreement being put into a subordinate clause. However for Luther the point of disagreement (on the bodily presence of Christ) was vital. It meant that he was unwilling to regard Zwingli as a brother and it prevented union between them.

Although the colloquy did not bring unity, it ended the bitter conflict. In this the mediating work of Bucer and Oecolampadius on the one side and of Melanchthon on the other was important. Nevertheless the absence of total agreement prevented an alliance with the Lutheran powers, which had become more pressing in the face of growing Catholic opposition, manifest at the Diet of Speyer in 1529 and the Diet of Augsburg in 1530. Zurich had, however, entered into alliance with Constance in 1527, with Berne and St Gallen in 1528, with Basle, Schaffhausen, Biel, and Mühlhausen in 1529, and with Hesse in 1530. (Already in 1524 the five cantons of Uri, Schwyz, Zug, Lucerne, and Unterwalden had entered into an alliance against the Reformation in Zurich, and in 1529 they made an alliance with King Ferdinand of Austria.) Zwingli was in fact prepared for alliances even with powers which were not Protestant but which were simply opposed to the emperor, in order to secure the preaching of the gospel.

Alliances meant a willingness that ultimately the sword should defend the preaching of the word. Zwingli was ready for this in 1529 and again in 1531. In 1529 peace was concluded with the five cantons without the decisive battle which would have been in Zurich's favour. The persecution of some followers of the Reformation that ensued made Zwingli urge invasion of the Catholic cantons. Berne however counselled sanctions, which Zwingli for his part regarded as unjust, because they involved the suffering of the innocent. Nevertheless they were agreed on, and there was an embargo on wheat, wine, salt, iron, and steel. Various attempts at negotiation failed. Eventually in October the forces of the five cantons assembled and on 9 October 1531 they crossed the borders of the canton of Zurich. Zurich itself was only twelve miles away. After a hasty meeting of the council an advance guard left the city. Battle began before the next contingent of 1,500 arrived. According to Swiss custom, Zwingli, as the chief pastor, bore the banner on horseback. He urged the 1,500 into battle to support the 1,200 already there.

But tired, ill-prepared, and outnumbered three to one, they could not prevail—and in the battle Zwingli was wounded and killed.

His death was seen by Luther as the judgement of God. Bucer was shocked by it, but a few days later he wrote to Melanchthon: 'He was a truly religious man, who believed in the Lord and also one who greatly loved good letters and furthered them among his own people.... In truth he looked to nothing other than the glory of Christ and the salvation of his native land.' (*ZWA* 14 (1978) 484.)

Zwingli's death and the defeat at Kappel on 11 October halted the Reformation in Switzerland for a time. But in Zurich the young Heinrich Bullinger succeeded him and developed the work which he had begun—and then a few years later in Geneva the Reformation drew new breath under the leadership of Calvin.

3

The Bible

THE Bible was at the heart of Zwingli's reformation. When he began his ministry in Zurich on his 35th birthday on 1 January 1519, he announced that the next day he would begin a continuous exposition of St Matthew. The dozen years that followed until his death in 1531 were remarkable for the central place given to the exposition and proclamation of the word. He preached regularly—not only in the Great Minster, but also on Fridays, market-day, in the Minster of our Lady. In the former he began by expounding St Matthew and the Acts of the Apostles and then in 1521–2 he continued with some of the epistles. Eventually he preached from most of the Bible, Old Testament as well as New. The preaching was practical and topical. It grappled not only with distinctively religious issues, but also with social and political ones.

The importance of the preaching of the word is evident in Zwingli's concern for freedom to preach the word in other cities and cantons as well. For example, the first condition for peace in the war of 1529 was freedom for the preaching of the word, and the alliances which he sought had the same concern. For Zwingli the word of God 'will as surely have its way as the Rhine, which you can stem for a while, but not stop' (Z III 488.7–8).

Behind Zwingli's preaching lay his study of scripture. It was in 1513 that the humanist priest in Glarus began to learn Greek in order to study the Bible. He immersed himself so deeply in the Greek text that in later years he most naturally quoted from the New Testament in Greek rather than in Latin or German. Indeed he copied the Pauline epistles in Greek and, it would seem from one reference, learned them by heart. Hebrew came with more difficulty than Greek. He started learning it before coming to Zurich, and began again in his first year there, in order to expound the Psalms in 1520. Yet on 25 March 1522 he wrote to Beatus Rhenanus in Basle, 'Greet Pellican and tell him I have begun Hebrew. Ye gods, what a distasteful and melancholy study! But I shall persist until I get something out of it.' (Z VII 497.27–29.) However 1522 was the year in which with the help of Böschenstein and Ceporinus he began to master the language.

His biblical study bore fruit in his debate with others and in the prophecy. Frequently in debate (as with Faber and Luther) he challenged his opponent's case by reference to the Greek or Hebrew text. However it was in the prophecy that his concern for the scholarly study of scripture is most evident. From June 1525 preachers and students met five times a week to study the Bible. The Old Testament was read first in Latin from the Vulgate, then in Hebrew, and finally in Greek from the Septuagint. The Hebrew and Greek were expounded in Latin, the language of the educated, before a final exposition in German, the language of the people. For Zwingli it was only by such a fundamental study of the scripture that the preaching of the church could be free from error, both the error of Catholics' appealing to tradition and the error of radicals' appealing to the Spirit. (For the anabaptist, Hubmaier, however, Zwingli was exchanging dependence on popes and councils for dependence on linguists.) The prophecy was of central importance in educating Reformed ministers, and through the years it also led to a series of valuable translations and commentaries (on Genesis, Exodus, Isaiah, Jeremiah, and the gospels), and in 1531 to the Zurich Bible.

Underlying the study of scripture and the preaching from it was the conviction that it was God's word. It was for this reason that it was central to Zwingli's reformation. That is why at the first disputation in January 1523 he could point to the Bible, which had been brought into the assembly in Hebrew, Greek, and Latin, as the judge. (Indeed the introduction to the sixty-seven articles which he was to defend at that disputation asserted that they were based on the Bible.) In all his debates Zwingli appealed to its authority and rejected the authority of the church and its traditional teaching. He invited his opponents to correct him from scripture, and made it clear that he was prepared to be in a minority of one, if he spoke with scripture and not against it.

The Authority of the Bible

The authority of the Bible lay in its being God's word, and Zwingli opposed this to man's word, as he opposed truth to error. The tradition of the church, even when expressed by councils or by the pope, was in the end man's word and not God's. In this conflict Zwingli frequently referred to Rom. 3:4, 'Let God be true, though every man be false.'

The Bible is God's word because it was spoken by God and because God speaks through it. 'The doctrine of God is never formed more clearly than when it is done by God himself and in the words of God.' (Z I 378. 17–18; LCC xxiv. 89–90.)

Zwingli maintained the unity and consistency of God's word. He did not allow any disharmony in scripture, but insisted on the agreement of its different parts, as they derive from the Spirit who is the Spirit of concord (Z V 735. 21–3). He therefore argued for the agreement of apparently inconsistent passages, just as, for example, Bucer did, although Bucer's treatment of such texts in his commentary on Romans was much more systematic. Nevertheless Zwingli was not a literalist, and he recognized minor differences between say Matthew and Mark. Although Zwingli stressed certain parts of scripture, calling St John the noblest part of the New Testament, he did not, unlike Luther, have a canon within the canon. His appeal, like that of Bucer and Calvin, was rather to the whole of scripture. At the same time, like Luther, he did not accept the Revelation of St John as canonical. Following Jerome, he thought it was not held as canonical in the early church. For him it lacked the heart and spirit of John.

He saw a fundamental difference between scripture and the tradition of the church. By contrast with scripture the utterances of the fathers, the councils, and the popes are human words.

Therefore in debate with his Catholic opponents he challenged the authority of the fathers, for 'the fathers must yield to the word of God and not the word of God to the fathers' (Z III 50. 5–9). The Bible is 'master, teacher, and guide', not the fathers (Z I 307. 1–4). In any case the councils and fathers were not always consistent, which means that they have to be tested by scripture and, as Zwingli put it, by Christ as the touchstone (Z I 302. 35–303. 10).

Yet Zwingli was not simply a man of one book: the Bible. He made use of fathers, councils, and popes to support his case and to show that his views were not his alone. He also used them in order to debate with his opponents on their own ground and to fight them with their own weapons. After citing a series of patristic texts in *A Commentary* he stated explicitly his reason for using the fathers:

> I have quoted these things from the weightiest of the fathers, not because I wish to support by human authority a thing plain in itself and confirmed by the word of God, but that it might be manifest to the feebler brethren that I am not the first to put forth this view, and that it does not lack very strong support (Z III 816.1–4: *Works* iii. 247–8).

This quotation from *A Commentary* occurs not surprisingly in a discussion of the eucharist, for that was the subject above all that caused Zwingli to examine the fathers in support of his case. As the years passed the range of quotations increased, with Augustine always of central importance theologically. (Overall there are twice as many references to Jerome as to Augustine, but that is because Jerome was used so often in the Old Testament commentaries on points of philology and exegesis.) In his dispute with Luther on the two natures of Christ, Zwingli argued that Luther's view of the two natures was contrary to that of the fathers, and indeed also to that of the schoolmen (Z V 943. 11–14).

Zwingli disallowed the appeal to councils, in part because of their inconsistency but more importantly because such an appeal subjects God's word to men, and therefore to those opposed to his word. 'To cry for councils is nothing but to cry for the word of God to be imprisoned again and imprisoned in the power of the swaggering bishops.' (Z II 449.17–19.)

An interesting example of his rejection of human authority comes in his dispute with Jerome Emser. Emser appealed to the way people have invoked the aid of St Nicholas in storms at sea. Zwingli rejected such an appeal by pointing out that Castor and Pollux have rescued many more from shipwreck and therefore ought to be invoked rather than Nicholas. He shows the futility of appealing to human authority, whether in tradition or experience, and makes his appeal to scripture which states that our help comes from God alone. (Z III 273.1–276.17.)

Yet, despite the centrality of scripture for Zwingli, there is a wide use of non-biblical writings, especially in two of his major works, *A Commentary* and *The Providence of God*. It is true that he could dismiss non-biblical writers with scorn, but he also used them in support of his argument. He claimed that he did this for the sake of those for whom he was writing, using—as he put it in his first reformation work—a heathen argument for the sake of those who were better versed in Aristotle than in the New Testament (Z I 98.3–6). Zwingli supported his use of non-biblical writers by the example of Paul in the New Testament (Acts 17: 28) and Jethro in the Old. 'Let us receive from them anything good or true that they have said and turn it to the glory of our God, and from the spoil of the Egyptians let us adorn the temple of the true God.' (Z XIII 382. 28–31.) In this use of non-biblical writers Zwingli stood in the tradition not only of his humanist contemporaries but also of many of the fathers. Following Jerome and Augustine, he asserted that 'all truth is of God'.

In *The Providence of God*, where the Bible is in the background and philosophical argument in the foreground, he defended his use of non-biblical testimony, such as Plato, Pythagoras, and Seneca, by asserting that 'writings are properly called sacred when they proclaim the thought of the holy, pure, eternal and infallible mind', adding that 'all that I have said and all that I am going to say in this book is derived from one source, namely from the nature and character of the Supreme Deity. This source Plato also tasted, and Seneca drank from it.' (Z VI

iii. 106.5–8, 106.16–107.1; *Works* ii. 151.) At the end of the work, however, Zwingli insisted that the foundation of his case was scripture, even though he had used philosophical arguments. This indicates that he saw the criterion of truth to be scriptural.

Zwingli undoubtedly used non-biblical writers more positively than Luther, but there is no sense in which non-biblical writings have independent authority. Indeed Christians are reminded of the biblical revelation and directed to go to it rather than to non-biblical writers. He stated this in *A Commentary* when he affirmed, 'But we, to whom God has spoken through his Son and through the Holy Spirit, are to seek these things not from those who were puffed up with human wisdom, and consequently corrupted what they received pure, but from the divine oracles' (Z III 643.24–7; *Works* iii. 62). Only of scriptural testimony did he say that it was 'unassailable' (S IV 56.18).

There is, however, an important difference with Luther here. Zwingli did not see as sharply as Luther did the uniqueness of the biblical revelation. This was in part because, like Augustine and Origen, he interpreted non-biblical writers in the light of scripture. Thus, for example, when they refer to gods in the plural, Zwingli took them to refer to the one God, just as the Hebrews did with the word elohim, which was also plural. There is therefore in Zwingli a considerable christianizing of non-biblical writers, which enabled him to treat them positively, while insisting on the authority of scripture.

The Interpretation of the Bible

The reformers shifted the starting-point of theological debate to the scripture. It alone was authoritative. They appealed to its clear testimony, but in doing so they were inescapably involved in discussion of its interpretation, not least when they used or interpreted passages of scripture differently from their opponents. In the course of controversy with his opponents (Catholic, radical, and Lutheran) Zwingli developed various principles of interpretation, of which the most fundamental was that scripture comes from the Spirit and can be understood aright only where the Spirit gives understanding.

He accused his Catholic opponents of using human reasoning to interpret scripture, so that they read out of it what human reason had first read into it. This was expressed clearly in one of his earlier works, *The Clarity and Certainty of the Word of God*, where he recognized in a measure the force of his opponents' case. 'I know that you will reply that you have worked through the scriptures and discovered texts which support your opinion.' (Z I 376. 15–17; LCC xxiv. 88.) For him his opponents misunderstood the scripture because they went to it to find support for their own views, whereas the right approach is:

> Before I say anything or listen to the teaching of man, I will first consult the mind of the Spirit of God (Ps. 84 [A.V. 85]): 'I will hear what God the Lord will speak.' Then you should reverently ask God for his grace, that he may give you his mind and Spirit, so that you will not lay hold of your own opinion but of his.... You must be *theodidacti*, that is, taught of God, not of men. (Z I 377. 7–20; LCC xxiv. 88–89.)

Without the Spirit people read their own ideas into scripture. Therefore before people approach scripture they need to pray to God, so that they may receive his mind and Spirit; otherwise they are blinded by the flesh or human reason. This does not mean that scripture is not clear; the problem is rather that we are not open or receptive to it. The necessity for the Spirit in understanding and interpreting scripture fits the God-centred character of Zwingli's theology. He never tires of quoting passages such as 'And they shall all be taught of God' (John 6: 45). This approach, with its emphasis on the role of the Spirit, leads Zwingli generally to speak of Spirit and Word, in contrast to Luther who spoke of Word and Spirit for without the Spirit we cannot understand the word.

The emphasis Zwingli gives to the Spirit does not, however, make the Spirit a substitute for scripture. He sees that as the error of some of the radicals, who appealed to the Spirit, although it was their own spirit rather than God's Spirit who inspired them.

For as often as by the use of clear passages of scripture they are driven to the point of having to say, I yield, straightway they talk about 'the Spirit' and deny scripture. As if indeed the heavenly Spirit were ignorant of the sense of scripture which is written under his guidance or were anywhere inconsistent with himself. (Z VI i. 24. 2–6; *Selected Works* 126.)

Luther's charge against Zwingli of being an enthusiast (*Schwärmer*) was exactly Zwingli's charge against Luther because—for Zwingli—Luther was arguing without the support of God's word. Zwingli used the analogy of a horse and reins, in which both are needed. The reins do not draw without the horse, but the reins keep the horse on the track. 'For it is no less agreeable and delightful than fair and just for us to submit our judgement to the holy scriptures, and the church, deciding in harmony with these by virtue of the Spirit.' (Z VI ii. 815.21–3; *Works* ii. 58.) As the Spirit is the author as well as the interpreter of scripture, his guidance is always in keeping with scripture.

The reformers read and were influenced by Augustine's *On the Spirit and the Letter*, and Zwingli was no exception. Augustine saw the fundamental distinction of letter and spirit in 2 Cor. 3: 6 not as between the literal and the figurative or spiritual meaning of a passage, but as between the letter and the Holy Spirit. He gave as an example of the letter that kills the command not to covet. It is to be taken literally. Yet taken literally, it kills, because we cannot keep it without the Holy Spirit who gives life. However not all passages are to be taken literally. Augustine also allowed the distinction between the literal and spiritual meaning and held that there were many passages, as in the Song of Songs, where we must look for the spiritual or figurative and not the literal meaning. These two senses of letter and spirit are evident in Zwingli. The probable impact of Erasmus is to be seen in the distinction he makes between the word and its sense or real meaning.

A proper understanding of scripture involved Zwingli, in common with his contemporaries, in using a number of principles of interpretation: setting disputed passages in their context, comparing one passage of scripture with another, and employing the various senses of scripture. The importance of context and comparison is evident in controversy, especially the eucharistic controversy. Thus Zwingli insisted that the crucial clause 'This is my body' must be seen in the context of the words that follow it: 'which is given for you' and 'Do this in remembrance of me'. It must also be compared with other passages of scripture such as 'The flesh is of no avail' (John 6: 63). Another form of comparison is in the use of analogy. The most important ones Zwingli used were between baptism and the eucharist in the New Testament and circumcision and the passover in the Old Testament. (Comparison was used to reconcile apparently conflicting passages, such as the statements on faith in James and Paul. Zwingli held that the passages must be in harmony, as the Spirit—and therefore scripture—is everywhere consistent.)

A further principle of interpretation is faith—in the sense of faith in God or in Christ rather than in ourselves. Like Augustine, Zwingli appealed to Isa. 7: 9, as translated in the Septuagint and the Vulgate, 'If you do not believe you will not understand.' He insisted that we learned by faith that flesh was not given to us to eat. Rather by faith we are sure that we are saved through Christ and that everything is given to us with him. What, he asked, could eating the flesh do in addition to that? He challenged Luther's appeal to the literal sense of the words 'This is my body' by reminding Luther of his own statement that a word is to be taken in its natural sense unless faith admonishes otherwise. (Z V 662.2–663.15.) It is faith which causes us not to interpret the words of institution literally any more than we should interpret literally (as Luther himself had argued) 'Upon this rock I will build my church'.

Faith as a principle of interpretation is frequently associated with love or the glory of God. To take from God his honour or glory and give it to anything else is for Zwingli the true idolatry.

In debate Zwingli appealed both to the Old Testament and the New. The theological priority lay with the New, even when he quoted Old Testament passages first, for his desire from the beginning was 'always to be guided by the scriptures of the New and Old Testament' (Z I 133.13–14). The Old Testament was to be read in the light of the New Testament, and not the New in the light of the Old. So, for example, Zwingli rejected arguments from the Old Testament that the eucharist is a sacrifice, as that is to turn from the light to the shadow. In a proper use of scripture you can find implicit in the Old Testament only what is explicit in Christ.

Against anabaptists, who insisted on arguing only from the New Testament, Zwingli had to defend his use of the Old. This was particularly important in the baptismal controversy, where anabaptists stressed the contrast between the Old and the New Testament. Against them he argued from the fact that Christ and the apostles appealed to the Old Testament. He quoted especially: 'Search the scriptures, in which you think you have eternal life, and they bear witness of me' (John 5: 39), 'Everything that was written was written for our instruction' (Rom. 15: 4), and 'Everything happened to them as a symbol, but was written for our instruction' (1 Cor. 10: 11).

There is a development in Zwingli's view of the Old Testament. In his earlier writing the emphasis was more on the contrast between the two testaments, in his later writings it was rather on the unity of the two. This shift in emphasis is related to the development in his understanding of the covenant. From 1525 he spoke of the one covenant which God had made, which was renewed in Christ. There is only one covenant, as there is only one God and one people of God. With this change in Zwingli's theology there was added further strength to the case he made against the anabaptists, as he was able to argue freely from both testaments.

In his interpretation of the Old Testament Zwingli stood in a tradition that went back to the fathers and to Philo. In this tradition various senses of scripture were distinguished—sometimes three, sometimes four. There were the three senses which Origen described as corporal (historical), psychical (moral), and spiritual (mystical), following his understanding of man as body, soul, and spirit. There were the four senses (literal, allegorical, tropological or moral, and anagogical) expressed in the thirteenth century in a couplet by the Dominican Augustine of Dacia. 'The literal sense (*littera*) teaches you what has happened, the allegorical what you should believe, the moral what you should do, and the anagogical what you should strive for.'

Zwingli's fundamental concern was with the natural sense. (However the natural sense can be seen as the spiritual sense, in that it comes not from human reason but from the Spirit who is the author of scripture.) This led to a detailed examination of the text, necessitating a knowledge of the biblical languages and of the Bible's many figures of speech. (Künzli has pointed to seventy rhetorical terms in the commentaries on Genesis and Exodus, and 200 in that on Isaiah.)[1] Especially in his commentaries on the prophets Zwingli drew heavily on Jerome in matters of language, history, and geography. A stress on the natural sense links Zwingli with the other reformers and also with medieval scholars such as Nicholas of Lyra.

Besides the natural sense is the moral sense. Texts such as 1 Cor. 10: 11 show that the Old Testament was written for our sake, but the same is true of the New Testament as well because for Zwingli there is nothing in the Bible that does not teach, admonish, or console (Z XIII 157.26–8). This moral purpose is furthered by the use of examples, and it all fits Zwingli's overall purpose in the study of the Bible. This was expressed in the prayer used at the beginning of the prophecy: 'open and illuminate our minds, that we may understand your oracles in a pure and holy way and be transformed into that which we have rightly understood' (Z IV 365.3–5).

In addition to the natural and moral sense, there is the mystical sense. This sense Zwingli saw as a biblical way of interpreting the Bible. He drew on Paul's words in 1 Cor. 10: 6 and 11, which speak of everything in the Old Testament as happening sybolically and as symbolizing something to us, as well as being written for us. For him the events were historical as well as symbolical, and he insisted on their historicity. However to see the promises of the prophets as having to do only with an earthly Israel or an earthly Jerusalem is to see them in a fleshly way as the Jews do. They also have an allegorical or symbolical sense.

[1] See E. Künzli, 'Zwingli als Ausleger von Genesis und Exodus', Diss. (Zurich, 1951), 57 and Z XIV 884.

The allegorical interpretation is related to the New Testament and above all to Christ, in keeping with his conviction that one must argue back from Christ who is the fulfilment of scripture. Only what is explicit in him may be read into a person or event in the Old Testament. In keeping with this Zwingli frequently used typology, with Noah, Isaac, Joseph, and Moses serving as types of Christ. Gen. 22, with its story of Abraham's sacrifice of Isaac, exemplifies various features in Zwingli's use of typology. It shows similarity: the three days correspond with Christ's resurrection on the third day, the ass with the ass ridden by Christ in entering Jerusalem, the wood borne by Isaac with the cross borne by Christ, and so on. Equally it shows dissimilarity: two boys compared with three disciples, showing the truth to be superior to the shadow, and Isaac's not dying, while Christ did die, for if Isaac had been like Christ in all things he would have been the truth and not the figure. (Z XIII 147.36–148.32.)

There are types or figures not only of Christ, but also of the church, evil powers, and the last things. Some are less compelling than others to the modern reader. In Gen. 32 the two feet of Jacob stand for the desire of the flesh and of the Spirit. The person who is lame in both feet, that is who desires at the same time to please God and the flesh, is accursed. The person who is lame in one foot, the flesh, so that he rests only on the Spirit and trusts in him alone, is happy. (Z XIII 213.8–12.) Faith, he says, teaches what things are to be understood typologically.

In the mystical sense of scripture Zwingli shows both a dependence on and an independence of Origen. He refers those who want more to Origen, but he also criticizes Origen for not treating a passage as historical. He gives a greater stress to the natural sense than Origen and is also more christological in his interpretation. For him, allegory is no more than a condiment to a meal. It is nothing by itself, but for the believer it can give a pleasant taste to something which has its basis in scripture.

The centrality of the Bible for Zwingli is evident in the three vital institutions of the Zurich Reformation: preaching, the disputations, and the prophecy. Each of them is an assertion of the authority of the Bible over against every other authority. Each of them, though especially the prophecy, shows him wrestling with the interpretation of the Bible. Each of them in its own way affirms the sovereignty of God, which underlies the whole of Zwingli's thought.

4

God: The Sovereignty of God

FOR Zwingli the life of the church and the teaching of the church had lost their centre in God. He was concerned to see that both theology and the Christian life recover that centre. In that sense the great reformation slogans were true for him: 'Christ alone', 'scripture alone', 'grace alone', 'faith alone'. But perhaps most characteristic of him would be 'God alone' or 'the honour or glory of God'.

In *A Commentary* in 1525 he expressed the character of true and false religion in this way:

> True religion, or piety, is that which clings to the one and only God. ... True piety demands, therefore, that one should hang upon the lips of the Lord and not hear or accept the word of any but the bridegroom. ... It is false religion or piety when trust is put in any other than God. They, then, who trust in any created thing whatsoever are not truly pious. They are impious who embrace the word of man as God's. (Z III 669.17–25, 674.21–4: *Works* iii. 92, 97–8.)

Zwingli's challenge was to a religion and theology where the centrality of God had been lost. In religion that meant placing one's trust in the creature rather than the creator; in theology it meant placing one's trust in human tradition and teaching rather than in God's word. This double challenge is characteristic of Zwingli's writings from beginning to end.

Zwingli's conviction of God's sovereignty or glory runs like a thread through the whole of his theology and colours every view which he presents. It finds most obvious expression in his understanding of providence and predestination. Nevertheless important as predestination was in the later Zwingli, it does not really feature in his writings until 1526—and then it is in response to the challenge of the anabaptists. Yet the sense of

God's providence is present in almost all of Zwingli's writings—and it is clearly both a personal experience and an intellectual conviction.

The Knowledge of God

The fundamental importance of the doctrine of God is apparent in Zwingli's systematic expositions of his thought. In *A Commentary* as in *An Account of the Faith* and *An Exposition of the Faith*, both of which are modelled on the creed, he begins with the doctrine of God. They affirm in their different ways the central place of God as opposed to all that is not God, the creator over against the creature.

It is, however, in his more systematic presentations of the faith that Zwingli is judged by some to be as much a philosopher as a theologian, as much dependent on non-biblical as on biblical sources. Certainly the humanist and scholastic influences permeate Zwingli's thought, even if they do not control it. Humanist influence is manifest in the place he gives to classical authors, especially Plato and Seneca, and scholastic influence is clear in the discussion of the knowledge of God (his existence as well as his nature). Both humanist and scholastic influences are evident in *A Commentary* and *The Providence of God*.

A Commentary begins with a discussion of the knowledge of God, in which Zwingli makes the traditional distinction between the knowledge of God's existence and the knowledge of his nature. He allows that most people have been aware of God's existence, but he does not regard the knowledge of God as inherent in people, but—in keeping with Paul in Rom. 1: 19—as coming from God. (Z III 640.28–644.18.) Religion, moreover, is not something natural to man, but rather dependent on God, for—in a reference to Adam—he says that it 'took its rise when God called runaway man back to him, when otherwise he would have been a deserter for ever' (Z III 667.9–12, 30–3; *Works* iii. 89–90).

The question naturally arises how this knowledge of God, which people can have independently of the incarnation, relates to Christ. Zwingli faced this question in *A Commentary* where he had given almost forty pages to a consideration of the nature of religion, God, and man, before turning to Christ and the gospel. In response to any who might say that he had made 'no reference to salvation through Christ and to grace' his defence was:

First, because I cannot say everything at once and in the same place; secondly, because all that I have said of the marriage of the soul to God applies to Christ just as much as to God (for Christ is God and man) and finally, because knowledge of God in the nature of the case precedes knowledge of Christ. (Z III 675.25–34; *Works* iii. 99.)

Locher takes this enigmatic sentence of Zwingli to mean that in order to understand who Christ is one must first know the doctrine of God as Father, Son, and Holy Spirit.[1] However it would be quite natural to take the sentence in the historical sense that God made himself known before he made himself known in Jesus Christ. Whichever view is right the problem of the starting-point in Zwingli's theology remains: God or God's revelation of himself in Jesus Christ.

In *A Commentary* Zwingli began with an exposition of the being of God and then considered his goodness. In *The Providence of God*, with its different subject, he began with God's goodness and then considered his being. In both, but especially the latter, the language of some of the discussion is philosophical or scholastic, with terms like entelechy and *summum bonum* (the highest good). Yet the basis of the discussion even in these works is biblical, despite the use of non-biblical sources and ideas, and that is certainly true in the writings that precede them. However for those who begin with these writings or concentrate their study of Zwingli on them, Zwingli will seem much more a philosopher than a biblical theologian.

The Providence of God

There were various influences at work in Zwingli's understanding of God's sovereignty. Apart from the Bible which was

[1] G. W. Locher, *Die Theologie Huldrych Zwinglis im Lichte seiner Christologie* (Zurich, 1952), 55 n. 14.

fundamental, there were Christian writers, especially Augustine, and non-Christian writers, especially Seneca. Besides these intellectual influences on Zwingli's thought, however, there was also the impact of Zwingli's personal experiences which are likely to have confirmed and indeed to have strengthened his understanding of God's sovereignty. He suffered from the plague in 1519 and later wrote a poem about it which expresses an utter trust in God and a powerful sense of being an instrument in the hands of God. The first section 'At the Beginning of the Illness' opens with the words:

Help, Lord God, help
In this trouble!
I think Death is at the door.
Stand before me, Christ;
For Thou hast overcome him!
To thee I cry:
If it is Thy will
Take out the dart,
Which wounds me
Nor lets me have an hour's
Rest or repose!
Will'st Thou however
That Death take me
In the midst of my days,
So let it be!
Do what thou wilt;
Me nothing lacks.
Thy vessel am I;
To make or break altogether.
(Z I 67.5–24; *Works* i. 56)

This trust in God is evident in Zwingli's letters. Thus in a letter to Myconius on 24 July 1520 he wrote: 'I beseech Christ for this one thing only, that he will enable me to endure all things courageously, and that he break me as a potter's vessel or make me strong, as it pleases him.' (Z VII 344.15–17; Jackson 148.) The sense of man's being a vessel in the hands of the potter is a recurring note in his works. He recognized God's providence not only in matters of life and death, but also in the events of every day. Thus in a letter to Vadian on 28 March 1524 he spoke of the immense pressure under which he worked, so that having to attend to the needs of people when he was writing meant that he forgot what he intended to write. Yet he added at once, 'In all these things I recognize the providence of God.' (Z VII 166.14–167.4.)

His own sense of the providence of God and the way he developed his understanding of providence in his early writings show that his affirmation of God's sovereignty and providence was nourished by the Bible and his personal experience. It was rooted in the sense of God's goodness revealed in Christ and found expression in his frequent reference to the questions in 8: 31–2: 'If God is for us, who is against us?' and 'He who did not spare his own Son but gave him up for us all, will he not also give us all things with him?' It was sustained by a range of biblical texts showing, as Jas. 1:17, that everything good comes from above, from the Father of light (Z II 96.27–34). It was expressed in the conviction not simply that all good comes from God, but that everything happens out of his providence and that not a sparrow falls to the ground without his ordaining it. After using this reference to Matt. 10: 28–31 in *An Exposition of the Articles*, Zwingli goes on to draw the conclusion that all our good works are therefore ordained by God and cannot be ascribed to us (Z II 178.32–179.20).

It is his belief in the sovereignty of God that is the weapon which Zwingli used against the belief of Erasmus and others in free will and merit. This is not the place to enter into the detailed case that Zwingli advanced, but in the course of it he argued that the believer knows that he is an instrument through whom God works and so he ascribes everything to God, whereas unbelievers, if they do apparently good works, ascribe them to themselves. The unbeliever, in other words, is incapable of grasping the sovereignty of God whereas the believer knows it from experience.

Initially references to the providence of God were primarily either in opposition to the doctrine of free will and merit, which would ascribe to man a part in his salvation, or in the believer's sense of utter dependence on God. However in his more detailed theological discussion in *A Commentary* Zwingli stressed the fact the everything in the universe is dependent on God as the sole cause, and that God would not be God, if anything lay outside his providence.

It is evident, therefore, that God ... is ... such wisdom, knowledge, and foresight that nothing is hidden from Him, nothing unknown to Him, nothing beyond His reach, nothing disobedient to Him. Hence not even the mosquito has its sharp sting and musical hum without God's wisdom, knowledge, and foresight. His wisdom, then, knows all things even before they exist, His knowledge comprehends all things, His foresight regulates all things. For that which is God would not be the supreme good unless he were at the same time supreme wisdom and foresight. (Z III 647. 7–16; *Works* iii. 66.)

So it is that he could say 'all things are so done and disposed by the providence of God that nothing takes place without His will or command' (Z III 842. 28–30; *Works* iii. 372).

Both *A Commentary* and *The Providence of God* show that Zwingli's method is sometimes as much logical as theological. In *A Commentary* he reached the point in the argument where he stated that 'it is time to bring forward the witness of the word itself to everything that has been said so far about the wisdom and providence of God'. However the biblical testimony is not an afterthought, for he held that 'the whole scripture of the Old Testament views everything as done by the providence of God'. (Z III 648.21–2, 649.1–3; *Works* iii. 68–9.) Rather Zwingli has followed the example of Paul in Rom. 1 in looking first at the world in which God has manifested himself. In this way he deliberately accommodated himself to those for whom he was writing.

The Providence of God, which is his major work on the subject, is the least biblical and most philosophical of all Zwingli's writings. He sought to make a logically coherent case for the doctrine of providence, beginning from the nature of God as the highest good. Thus his first thesis was 'Providence necessarily exists, because the highest good necessarily cares for and orders all things.' (Z VI iii. 70.7–8; *Works* ii. 130.) Although there is no fundamental change in Zwingli's understanding of providence, the nature of the argument and the non-biblical presentation of the doctrine mark this discussion off from the earlier ones. Zwingli admitted that he 'made larger use of argument than of the testimony of scripture' though that was 'the foundation for the whole argumentation' (Z VI iii. 229.20–230.4; *Works* ii. 233). He consciously used a philosophical approach, on the basis that all truth is of God, and cited as witnesses Plato and Seneca alongside Moses and Paul (Z VI iii. 83.15–16), while drawing also on Aristotle, Pliny, Plutarch, and Pythagoras.

Zwingli's deep humanist roots are evident here. Yet even this strongly philosophical case for providence does not mean that Zwingli's view of God was more philosophical than biblical, though some have taken that view. His position was derived from scripture and shaped by his own experience of God. The assertion of God's providence is set over against any other cause whether, as for many at that time, chance or human action, for a so-called secondary cause is no more than a means or instrument in God's hands. His fundamental concern was to ascribe glory to God.

Belief in the providence or sovereignty of God did not lead to resignation but rather to a trusting submission to God. It did not lead, as one might suppose, to passivity, with everything being left to God, but rather to activity, to a sense of being an instrument for good in the hand of God.

Predestination

Important as predestination became for Zwingli, it did not develop as an independent doctrine until 1526. Before that it was included in his understanding of God's providence and indeed he could speak of providence as 'the mother of predestination, as it were' (Z III 842.9–11; *Works* iii. 271). Many of the issues which were later related to predestination (such as free will and merit) were dealt with initially in the context of God's sovereignty or providence.

In 1526, however, he made use of the doctrine of election in the controversy about baptism, particularly infant baptism. In *Original Sin* he attacked those who bound salvation to baptism, since it comes 'to those elected of God, not to those who do this or that', and they were elected before they were born (Z V 378.2–5; *Works* ii. 11). He criticized those who regarded Gentiles or the unbaptized children of Christians as damned, arguing that Christ did not say, 'He who is not baptized will not be saved.' (The reference is to the words in Mark 16: 16: 'He who believes and is baptized will be saved; but he who does not believe will be condemned.') Zwingli's use of this text in Mark 16 was challenged by Urbanus Rhegius in favour of linking salvation and faith as in Heb. 11: 6, a link Zwingli himself had made in *An Exposition of the Articles* (Z II 426.19–25). Zwingli insisted that these passages apply to those hearing the word and not to children. Faith is a sign of election in adults, but its absence in children is not a sign that they will be damned (Z VIII 737.7–738.27).

The argument from election then became a major argument in Zwingli's attack on the anabaptists, though they seem to have taken the initiative in introducing it into the debate with him by their reference to Rom. 9: 11–13. Zwingli used this passage in *A Refutation* in 1527 to underline his position that the absence of faith does not necessarily imply that a person is not elect, for—as with Jacob—the elect are always elect before they believe. Zwingli was aware of the danger that too great a stress on election could diminish or eliminate the role of Christ in salvation. He insisted, however, that the elect are destined to be saved through Christ (Z VI i. 181.19–22).

It is in *The Providence of God* that Zwingli engaged in his most sustained treatment of predestination or election, and it is again clear that his emphasis is on election rather than reprobation, even if the one implies the other. He preferred the word election to the word predestination; moreover he spoke of election as originating in the goodness of God, which here and in some other places embraced both God's righteousness and his mercy. It is not as if election proceeds from God's mercy and reprobation from his righteousness. (Z VI iii. 150.3–152.12.)

In his concern to insist that election is entirely of God and has nothing to do with our works, Zwingli stressed that election comes from God's will rather than from his wisdom, although for Zwingli God's attributes cannot be separated. He opposed the opinion, as Calvin did later, that God elects someone when he foresees by his wisdom what he will be like. (Z VI iii. 155.22–165.4.) That view makes election and therefore salvation dependent on man rather than on God.

Zwingli discussed the question of whether we can know that we and others are elect, an issue that was to become prominent in Reformed and Puritan circles. He was not primarily concerned, as many were later, with our knowing whether or not we or others are elect. He was rather concerned to attack the idea that salvation depends on our faith or love, insisting that faith and love depend on God's election. Nevertheless he does assert that we can know from our works and love as well as from our faith that we are elect. At some points he regards faith and good works (or their absence) as evidence that others are elect (or not), but at other points he recognizes the need for caution, for we can be mistaken as we are able to judge others only by appearance. In *An Account of the Faith* where he discussed election in the context of the church which is without spot or wrinkle and known only to God, he wrote, 'those who are members of this church, since they have faith, know that they themselves are elect and are members of this church, but are ignorant of the members other than themselves' (Z VI ii. 800.19–35; Jackson 463; *Works* ii. 43–4). Such caution is in keeping with the acknowledgement that there can be sin in the elect, as there was, for example, with David and the thief on the cross.

Zwingli's approach is, however, much less cautious in *An Exposition of the Faith*. In a work dedicated to the King of France he had a vision of heaven which included by name not only some of the patriarchs, prophets, and apostles, but also the king's predecessors ('the Louis, Philips, Pepins'), as well as non-Christians such as Hercules and Theseus (S IV 65.26–41; LCC xxiv. 275; *Works* ii. 272). Although Zwingli introduced important qualifying references to faith and goodness, yet his own view expressed only a few pages before was that 'the election and faith of others is always concealed from us, although the Spirit of the Lord gives us certainty of our faith and election' (S IV 61.3–6; LCC xxiv. 269; *Works* ii. 264).

The reference to non-Christians in heaven outraged Luther. For him it called in question the relationship between salvation and Christ. Zwingli always affirmed the necessity of Christ and of his death for our salvation. However the strong place in his theology given to election (as to the sovereignty of God) does lead to a different emphasis on or understanding of both Christ and word and sacrament than what we find in Luther.

The sovereignty of God is a motif running through the whole of Zwingli's theology, but it also raises questions, as we shall see, about the role of Christ in salvation as well as the role of word and sacrament.

5

Christ: Salvation in Christ

IT is in the way they understood and preached Christ and in particular salvation in Christ that the reformers differed most decisively from their opponents in the medieval church. Yet they differed also from each other in some of their emphases and interpretations. Some of these differences account in part for the disagreement between Zwingli and Luther.

One accent that is stronger in Zwingli than in Luther is the stress on Christ as teacher and example. This probably comes from the influence of Erasmus. Yet this does not deny the fundamental stress in Zwingli on him as saviour and as Son of God, but it does colour it. (It should be noted that Christ is said to be our teacher and example as Son of God, and not—as one might expect—as man.) The stress on him as God also leads to some of Zwingli's differences with Luther including the way he related the divinity of Christ to his humanity and the way he related Christ to the salvation of non-Christians. There are differences between them both in their understanding of the place of Christ and in their understanding of his person and work.

The Place of Christ

If the starting-point of Zwingli's more systematic works is God rather than Jesus Christ, that is not true of his most comprehensive work in German, *An Exposition of the Articles*. The central place of Christ is evident in the opening articles of the first disputation in 1523, though some see in this the influence of Luther at that time. The central concern is the gospel which is summarized in Christ. He is described among other things as the only way of salvation. Indeed all of the first twenty-three articles are related to Christ.

Yet in spite of the indispensable, and in many ways central, place Christ had for Zwingli, he was not the beginning, middle, and end of Zwingli's theology as he was of Luther's. Moreover the Christ on whom Zwingli concentrated was Christ as God rather than as man.

The central place of Christ derived from Zwingli's reading of a poem of Erasmus.

> I do not want to keep from you, most beloved brethren in Christ Jesus, how I have come to the opinion and firm faith, that we need no mediator except Christ, and that between God and us no one can mediate except Christ alone. Some eight or nine years ago I read a comforting poem of the most learned Erasmus of Rotterdam, addressed to the Lord Jesus, in which Jesus laments in many beautiful words that we do not seek all that is good from him although he is the source of all good, a saviour, comfort, and treasure of the soul. Then I thought: It is always so. Why do we seek help in the creature? (Z II 217.5–14.)

It is characteristic of this sense that Christ is the centre of Christian faith that one of the texts which Zwingli used most frequently and one which appeared on the title-page of his writings was Matt. 11: 28: 'Come to me, all who labour and are heavy laden, and I will give you rest.'

His exposition of Dan. 7: 25 saw Christ as exactly at the mid-point between creation and the end of the world. That places him at the centre. Nevertheless the way Zwingli spoke of those who lived before Christ or without knowledge of him raises questions about the centrality and indispensability of Christ, and in particular of his death and resurrection.

In what he said about the salvation of believers in the Old Testament Zwingli stood clearly in the tradition of the fathers. For him, as for Augustine, they believed in the Christ who is to come, whereas Christians believe in the Christ who has come. However although Zwingli stressed the difference between the Old and New Testaments, as well as their similarity, the emphasis shifted to the latter in the middle of the 1520s. In the controversy with the anabaptists he made increasing use of the fact that God made a covenant with his people of old, which was not abrogated but renewed in Christ.

In *A Refutation*, written against anabaptists, he asked the question: 'What difference is there between the Old and the New Testaments?' His response was:

Very much and very little, I reply. Very little if you regard those chief points which concern God and us; very much if you regard what concerns us alone. The sum is here: God is our God; we are his people. In these there is the least, in fact, no difference. The chief thing is the same today as it ever was. For just as Abraham embraced Jesus his blessed seed, and through him was saved, so also today we are saved through him. But so far as human infirmity is concerned, many things came to them in a figure to instruct them and be a testimony to us. These are therefore the things which seem to distinguish the Old Testament from the New, while in the thing itself or in what pertains to the chief thing they differ not at all. (Z VI i. 169.19–30; *Selected Works* 234.)

The problem is more acute with Gentiles, both those who lived before Christ and those who lived after him, than it is with Jews living before Christ. For Gentiles who lived before Christ, the Old Testament provided both examples, such as Jethro, Moses' father-in-law, and arguments. Thus Zwingli argued from Mal. 1: 11 that Gentiles before Christ sacrificed to the one true God. ('For from the rising of the sun to its setting my name is great among the nations, and in every place incense is offered to my name, and a pure offering, for my name is great among the nations, says the Lord of hosts.' (Mal. 1: 11).) Their sacrifices are related to the one sacrifice of Christ. (Z III 202.35–204.15.)

Zwingli was aware of the problems with his position and, after making a very positive reference to Seneca in *Original Sin*, he added: 'Who, pray, wrote this faith upon the heart of man? Let no one think that these things point to the taking away of Christ's office, as some men charge me with doing; they magnify his glory. For through Christ must come all who come to God.' (Z V 379.22–9; *Works* ii. 12–13.) Following Augustine he argued that Gentiles who show by their works that the law is written in their hearts have faith. They do the law by grace, or by faith, or by the Spirit of God (for these, in effect, say the same), and are to be counted among those justified by the Spirit of Christ. (S VI i. 242.6–243.1.)

Zwingli insisted on the necessity of Christ and his death for the salvation of all, but he did not relate this necessarily—as Luther would—to the proclamation of Christ and his saving death in word and sacrament. He based his understanding of the position of Gentiles on the evidence in scripture of what God has done in some of them and on the implications of his understanding of God's sovereignty in election. God's sovereignty is not limited historically to Israel. The Spirit created the whole world and is not therefore limited to Israel, but produces piety in those he elects, wherever they are. In that sense a Gentile 'is a Christian even if he does not not know Christ'. He argues for this, in part by analogy with the person in Rom. 2: 28–9 who is a Jew, not because of outward circumcision, but because of circumcision of the heart. (Z IX 458.25–459.7.)

The vision of heaven in *An Exposition of the Faith* which includes pious pagans is not however the product of a humanist universalism, as some have supposed. That would put the emphasis on their works or free will. For Zwingli their enjoyment of eternal life in God's presence is the fruit both of God's election, which was manifested in their piety (and not dependent on it), and of Christ's redemption of mankind, which reaches as far as Adam's fall did and therefore reaches all mankind.

The Person and Work of Christ

The place of Christ in salvation is related to his person, in particular his divinity, and to his work, in particular his sacrificial death. Zwingli frequently offered summaries of the gospel, as in the second of the sixty-seven articles, which included two vital elements: that Christ was Son of God and that he died for us, thereby satisfying the righteousness of God.

The primary understanding of Christ's death is that of Anselm, even though other elements are present. There is on occasion an almost Abelardian sense of the compelling power of God's love displayed in Jesus Christ. There is the Irenaean understanding of Christ as recapitulating all that happened in Adam. There is, following Athanasius, the view that Christ became human, so that we might become divine. There is also the presentation of Christ's death as a victory over or liberation from sin, death, and the devil. Yet the dominant note is the Anselmian one.

For Zwingli we have failed to keep God's law, indeed cannot keep it, because we are sinners, and therefore deserve his punishment. He is righteous and cannot simply pass over sin. In his mercy, however, he sent his Son who accomplished God's will and satisfied God's righteousness with his innocence. (Z II 36.25–39.19.)

God's work of election and salvation is related not only to his mercy or goodness, but also to his justice. 'It is of his goodness that he has elected whom he will; but it is of his justice to adopt and unite the elect to himself through his Son, who has been made a victim for satisfying divine justice for us.' (Z VI ii.796.25–30.) For Zwingli Christ's sacrificial death was the way God had determined to reconcile the world to himself and he regarded it as sacrilege to enquire whether it could have been done differently (Z V 391.20–2; *Works* ii. 27).

He is our salvation because he is both God and man. Zwingli expressed this in a variety of ways. In expounding the sixty-seven articles he wrote that as Christ is God, he can fulfil the will of God, as he is man he can be a sacrifice that satisfies the righteousness of God (Z II 182.5–13). In his Berne sermon he stated that as the godhead cannot suffer, the humanity was necessary, for it could suffer; yet at the same time no man can satisfy the righteousness of God, but only God (Z VI i. 464.5–17).

The stress on Christ's sacrificial death led to an emphasis on the virgin birth. The virgin birth was necessary, as Christ's divine nature could not suffer the stain of sin, but also the human nature had to be pure if it was to be the means of satisfying God's righteousness, for in the Old Testament the sacrificial victim was without stain.

And this could not have been unless he had been born of a virgin, and without male intervention. For if the virgin had conceived from the seed of a man, would not the birth have been thereby polluted? And if a woman who had before known a man had conceived him, even from the Holy Spirit, who would ever have believed that the child that was born was of the Holy Spirit? (Z III 686.7–28; *Works* iii. 112.)

Zwingli held that Mary was perpetually a virgin on the basis of passages such as Ezek. 44: 2: 'This gate shall remain shut, it shall not be opened, and no one shall enter by it, for the Lord the God of Israel, has entered by it, therefore it shall remain shut.' However he did not support devotion to Mary. Her role, like that of every Christian, was to point to Christ. Therefore he could say that the greatest honour we can give to Mary is to honour her Son. (Z I 426.5–427.9.)

There is in Zwingli a strong sense of the distinctiveness of the divine and human natures in Christ, which was to have a strong influence in later Reformed theology. It is clearly in the tradition of the Tome of Leo and the Council of Chalcedon, but nevertheless it led to accusations of Nestorianism. However Zwingli always insisted on the unity of the person of Christ as well as the distinction of the natures. It is not 'as if we wish to separate the natures in Christ, for the one Christ is God and man, but we desire rightly to distinguish between the works and properties of each nature and not to confound them'. (S VI i. 311.8–9, 357.15–28.)

The sharp distinction between the natures is one of the underlying reasons for Zwingli's and Luther's differences in understanding the Lord's Supper. For Zwingli Christ could not be present according to his human nature in the eucharist, because his human nature—like ours—can be in only one place. Only his divine nature can be present everywhere. Luther's stress lay on the unity of Christ's person, rather than the distinction of his natures. For him, therefore, wherever Christ is present he is present in both his natures, otherwise his person would be divided.

In the debate between them they both drew on analogies. Zwingli drew on two from the fathers, his preference being for that of soul and body, an analogy used by Cyril of Alexandria and Augustine, as well as the Athanasian Creed. Man is both soul and body, though soul and body are two opposed substances. Similarly the one Christ is both God and man. He also used the analogy of a red-hot sword (from Origen and John of Damascus), which cuts and burns, and disputed Luther's use of this analogy in support of his view of Christ's presence. (Luther used it to show that both Christ and bread can be present in the eucharist, just as two substances, that is fire and iron, are present in a red-hot sword.) Another of Zwingli's analogies was that of the sun, where the body is in one place and yet the light shines everywhere. With these analogies he sought to hold to the unity of the person of Christ and the distinction of his natures.

Zwingli supported his view of the sharing or interchange of properties (*communicatio idiomatum*) especially from John's gospel. For this he often used the rhetorical term alloiosis: 'where we name the one nature and understand the other, or name what they both are and yet understand only the one' (Z V 926.1–3). For him passages like John 3: 13; 6: 62; 10: 30; and 12: 25, 28 make sense only as they apply either to the humanity or to the divinity of Christ. One example from the controversy shows something of the way Zwingli argued here. Thus he challenged Luther to say whether 'Before Abraham was I am' applied to the humanity as well as to the divinity. If Luther said no, then alloiosis would be established. If he said yes, then Christ was not born of Mary, as she was not born before Abraham; or else Christ has two human natures, one before Abraham and one from Mary. (Z VI ii. 138.18–139.7.)

Zwingli was concerned that Luther was limiting God by confining him to Christ and enclosing him within the humanity of Christ, whereas he is infinite (Z V 934.11–936.10). Zwingli argued that Christ was concerned to safeguard the divine by refusing to accept the word good when it was used of him, for the person using it saw him only as man and not as God (Z V 700.1–17). The same kind of concern was seen in the words. 'He who believes in me, believes not in me but in him who sent me.' Here Christ was saying that trust belonged to him as God but not as man. Zwingli saw Luther by contrast as attributing to Christ's humanity the infinity which Christ refused, and in effect of teaching that trust should be put in the creature rather than the creator. (Z V 687.21–34.)

The humanity of Christ does not have the vital place in Zwingli's theology that it has in Luther's, even though it is indispensable for our salvation, for the stress is on the divinity which saves us and in which we are to put our trust. At points a sense of the genuine humanity of Christ is missing. For example, Jesus prayed not because he needed to, but as an example to us, and he asked questions not in order to learn, but to give us an example (S VI i. 480.28; Z III 726.33–7). Yet there are also occasions when Zwingli recalled the earthly life of Christ with great vividness; and his role as our example, derived in part from Erasmus, was always important.

There are differences between Zwingli and Luther not only in their understanding of the person of Christ (for example, Zwingli's stress on the distinctiveness of the natures and Luther's on the unity of the person) but also on their understanding of his place. The second of these has a bearing on their doctrine both of the Spirit and of word and sacrament.

6

The Holy Spirit: The Spirit and the Word

THE emphasis on the Spirit in Zwingli corresponds in part to the stress on Christ's divinity rather than his humanity. It reflects the emphasis on the centrality and sovereignty of God and the contrast (or opposition) between God and man in Zwingli's theology. The need, for example, to be taught of God was on occasion present in terms of being taught by the Spirit of God or the Holy Spirit, even where there is no mention of the Spirit in the biblical texts referred to.

The central role of the Spirit is evident in descriptions of Zwingli's theology as spiritualist or pneumatological. Some see it as spiritualist, as indeed Luther did, because for them the Spirit in Zwingli is not closely tied to the Word, but is rather independent of the Word. Others see it as pneumatological, because for them the Spirit is interpreted biblically and set in the context of the trinity. Both these descriptions have force.

An examination of the Spirit in Zwingli shows that he does not use the term vaguely as a synonym for God, but the Spirit is the Holy Spirit, related to Christ in the way that the Spirit is related to Christ in the New Testament. In this sense Zwingli's theology is pneumatological.

There are also, however, senses in which his theology may be described as spiritualist. It gives a priority to the Spirit, so that Zwingli naturally spoke of the Spirit and the Word, rather than the Word and the Spirit. Moreover there is in Zwingli a certain opposition between the Spirit and outward means, related to the Platonist contrast of flesh and spirit. Yet there is an injustice in using the term spiritualist for Zwingli, as the term covers an enormous diversity of people, and someone like Sebastian

Franck, for whom it is used, is farther from Zwingli than Zwingli is from Luther at these points.

For Franck there is an opposition between the Spirit and the Word or between the inward and outward word which is not to be found in Zwingli. This is evident in Franck's letter from Strasbourg to John Campanus in 1531, in which he stressed the Spirit in contrast to the written word of the scripture.

I should wish, however, that thou wert not so addicted to the letter of Scripture, thus withdrawing thy heart from the teaching of the Spirit, that thou wouldst not drive out the Spirit of God as though it were Satan, crowding him against his will into the script and making Scripture thy god (which has often happened and still happens). Thou shouldst much rather interpret the Scripture as a confirmation of thy conscience, so that it testifies to the heart and not against it. Again, thou shouldst not believe and accept something [merely] reported by Scripture—and feel that the God in thy heart must yield to Scripture. It were better that Scripture should remain Antichrist's! (LCC xxv. 159.)

It was precisely such a separation of the Spirit and scripture that Zwingli attacked in the anabaptists.

Franck also opposed the Spirit to the sacraments (or visible words) as a perversion of the true spiritual worship intended by God and enjoyed in the New Testament period.

Along with this, I ask what is the need or why should God wish to restore the outworn sacraments and take them back from Antichrist, yea, contrary to his own nature (which is Spirit and inward) yield to weak material elements? For he had been for fourteen hundred years now himself teacher and baptizer and governor of the Feast, that is, in that Spirit, I say, in order that he may baptize, instruct, and nourish our spirit. And does he wish now, just as though he were weary of Spiritual things and had quite forgotten his nature, to take refuge again in the poor sick elements of the world and re-establish the besmirched holy days and the sacraments of both Testaments? But God will remain [true] to his character, especially [as disclosed] in the New Testament, as long as the world stands. (LCC xxv. 154.)

This is a world away from Zwingli, who does not divorce the Spirit from the sacraments. Rather the Spirit sometimes works with them and sometimes without them.

There were contexts in which Zwingli spoke of the Spirit without relating him to God's revelation of himself in Jesus Christ. In some respects, at least, this reflects the use of the Bible or one way in which it can be interpreted. There are references to the Spirit as the Creator Spirit (as in Gen. 1), who created the whole universe and not only Palestine and so he is not limited to Palestine in his continuing work (Z IX 458.25–459.10). There are references to the Spirit as at work in the writing of the law in the hearts of those who are not Christians, as in Rom. 2: 14–15. Zwingli followed Augustine in understanding the law of nature in terms of the Spirit. (Z II 634.10–34, 327.3–7.) However the work of the Spirit in non-Christians is related to Christ as they were elected in Christ before the foundation of the world.

The Spirit is related to the word: the incarnate word, the written word, and the audible and visible word. The Spirit is related specifically to Christ, both to his birth and life and to his death and resurrection. More particularly he is seen as given at Pentecost in the place of Christ. The Spirit was sent by Christ and it is by the Spirit that Christ is now present and active. (Z II 80.15–16.) The text, 'I will not leave you orphans', is paraphrased in part in the words: 'Then after the ascension I will be present with you in my Spirit.' In his exposition of John 14: 26 Zwingli goes beyond the text in declaring that the Spirit will teach nothing new, as he brings to remembrance what Christ taught the disciples. (S VI i. 751.41, 752.41–4.) These passages show that the Spirit is bound closely to Christ in Zwingli's earlier and later writings.

The link of the Spirit with the written word of scripture is strong. He is the author of scripture, though not in a way that denies the individuality of the gospel writers. Zwingli noted the differences, even the inconsistencies, in the gospels but they did not trouble him, as faith does not depend on such things (S VI ii. 70.37–38). Errors, however, were never present in the substance or the essential matter (*in re*), but only in questions concerning people and times (Z XIII 41.31–2). In general, however, the differences were regarded as only apparent, and they were reconciled on the assumption that the true author is the Spirit, who does not contradict himself (Z V 735.21–23).

Zwingli's insistence on the divine origin and authority of scripture was most evident in his controversies with Catholics and anabaptists. Against Catholics he appealed to it as God's word, in contrast to the human words to which they appealed—the words of the pope or the councils or the fathers of the church. Against the anabaptists he appealed to it as God's word to confute their appeal to the Spirit speaking in them, for Zwingli saw this as their spirit and not the Holy Spirit. In both cases the authority of scripture lay in its origin in the inspiration of the Holy Spirit.

Yet Zwingli did not limit the Spirit to scripture. When writing against the anabaptists in *A Refutation* he refers to God's speaking 'also through sibyl prophetesses among the Gentiles, that we might recognize the liberty of his will and the authority of his election' (Z VI i. 162.8–11; *Selected Works* 226–7). However in *A Commentary* where he drew particularly on non-biblical writers, he directed attention to scripture with the statement, 'But we, to whom God has spoken through his Son and through the Holy Spirit are to seek these things not from those who were puffed up with human wisdom, and consequently corrupted what they received pure, but from the divine oracles' (Z III 643.24–7; *Works* iii. 62).

It is in the relation of the Spirit to word and sacrament that Zwingli is most often thought of as a spiritualist, for dissociating the Spirit from the word. Two distinct elements in Zwingli's thought combine to do this. The first is the freedom and sovereignty of the Spirit, and the second is a Platonist opposition of spirit and flesh in his understanding of man.

The freedom of the Spirit is affirmed in the frequent reiteration of 'The Spirit blows where he will' (John 3: 8) and 'It is the Spirit who gives life, the flesh is of no avail' (John 6: 63). He is not bound to word and sacrament, so that he must act through them or so that he cannot act apart from them. To assert the contrary is to put salvation at man's disposal, for it would mean that salvation could be guaranteed simply by hearing the word, or being baptized, or receiving holy communion; but equally it could mean that salvation could be denied by failure to preach the word or administer the sacraments.

For Zwingli, by contrast, the word of the teacher is of no avail unless the listener is taught of God. 'Even if you hear the gospel of Jesus Christ from an apostle, you cannot act upon it unless the heavenly Father teach and draw you by the Spirit' (Z I 366.30–3; LCC xxiv. 79). The word of the preacher, indeed the word of the human Jesus, is of no avail unless the Father draws the hearer. The flesh or body of the earthly Jesus, just as the flesh or body of Christ in the sacrament, is of no avail, for it is the Holy Spirit who gives life. In the end word and sacrament guarantee nothing. They are not automatically effective or effective for all because the Spirit blows where he wills, and you cannot make him blow simply by your act of preaching or baptizing or offering the sacramental bread.

For in this way the liberty of the divine Spirit who distributes himself to individuals as he wills, that is, to whom he wills, when he wills, where he wills, would be bound. For if he were compelled to act within when we employ the signs externally, he would be absolutely bound by the signs. (Z III 761.4–8; *Works* iii. 183.)

Word and sacrament are ineffective without the Spirit, but the Spirit is not ineffective without them. He does not need them, though they need him.

Moreover a channel or vehicle is not necessary to the Spirit, for he himself is the virtue and energy whereby all things are borne, and has no need of being borne; neither do we read in the holy scriptures that perceptible things, as are the sacraments, bear certainly with them the Spirit, but if perceptible things have ever been borne with the Spirit, it has been the Spirit, and not perceptible things, that has borne them. ... Briefly, the Spirit blows wherever he wishes. (Z VI ii. 803.10–22; Jackson 466–7; *Works* ii. 46.)

The other element in Zwingli's thought is his partially Platonist view of man, which is part of his humanist inheritance. This presupposes a sharp contrast or opposition between the inward and the outward, so that what is inward (the heart or mind) cannot be affected by what is outward (words, water, bread, and wine). What is outward appeals to and affects the outward. This factor is important, but it is less fundamental than the sovereign freedom of the Spirit, for that is the heart of

Zwingli's understanding of Christian theology, which is theocentric, and of Christian life, which involves faith in the creator rather than the creature.

If there is a dissociating of the Spirit from word and sacrament, there is also an associating of them. The natural order is nevertheless Spirit and Word, with the stress on the Spirit. In *The Clarity and Certainty of the Word of God*, where some see the strong influence of Luther, Zwingli emphasizes the word. He writes, 'The word of God is so sure and strong that if God wills all things are done the moment he speaks his word.' But even here the power of the word is set within the sovereignty of God's will, and when Zwingli discusses the clarity of the word he emphasizes the role of the Spirit, as the word is understood not because of human understanding, but because of 'the light and Spirit of God, illuminating and inspiring the words'. (Z I 353.8–13, 365.14–21; LCC xxiv. 68, 78.)

In expounding Isa. 59: 21 where the order is Spirit and word Zwingli stressed that the Spirit is placed first, for without the Spirit the flesh misunderstands the word. The church therefore has both the word preached by the prophets and the Spirit who illuminates where he wills. (Z XIV 391.1–7.) Where Zwingli contrasts the Spirit and the word his concern is often to affirm the Spirit rather than to deny the place of the word. Without the Spirit teaching inwardly, the outward word is in vain, for everyone must be taught of God. 'Yet it does not follow for that reason that the outward word is not necessary, for Christ commanded the apostles to preach the gospel through all the world.' (S VI i. 752.44–8.) There is no sense in which we can simply rely on the Spirit and dispense with the word. For, as he made clear in *A Commentary*, 'we are to be taught outwardly by the word of God and inwardly by the Spirit' (Z III 900.6–7).

There is a certain irony in the fact that the Marburg article on the outward word, drawn up by Luther, has a Zwinglian emphasis in making the Spirit the source of faith. Indeed it is a statement which Zwingli could well have written both with its affirmation that ordinarily the Spirit does not give faith to anyone without the word, and with its conclusion that the Spirit creates faith where and in whom he wills. (Z VI ii. 522.12–17.)

7

Salvation

AT the heart of the Reformation was the question of salvation. It was, of course, central in medieval theology and medieval religion, and it was against that background that the reformers formulated their understanding of salvation. Although there was fundamental agreement on this central element in their teaching, there were some important differences. These reflect their different theological traditions and the different ways they came to faith in Christ. For Zwingli the role of Erasmus and Erasmian humanism was an important factor both in his path to faith and in his theological development, although it was not the only one.

The turning-point for Zwingli was in 1515–16. He dated it from his reading of a poem of Erasmus. This led him to see that there is no mediator between God and man except Christ, who is our saviour, and to contrast this with seeking help in created things, whether they be saints or sacraments or good works.

Seven years later, when Zwingli presented for debate sixty-seven theses, which summarized what he had been preaching on the basis of scripture, the message was in a similar though maturer form. Articles fifty and fifty-one were: 'God remits sin only through Jesus Christ, His Son, our Lord', 'Whoever ascribes this to the creature, deprives God of his glory and gives to him who is not God; that is veritable idolatry.'

Zwingli's grasp of the gospel almost certainly developed in the years before he came to Zurich and in his first years in Zurich, but there is a fundamental continuity in his view. Beatus Rhenanus referred to his witty preaching in Einsiedeln with its attacks on ceremonies. His comments have been interpreted as meaning that Zwingli was a typically Erasmian preacher at that time, and no more. (That is possible. Yet it must be remembered that years later Bucer could speak of Erasmus as initiating the Reformation by his opposition to man's finding salvation in ceremonies and not in Christ.) It could be that he heard only what confirmed his own position and missed the characteristically reformation notes in Zwingli's preaching, but it is probable that throughout the years between 1516 and 1522 Zwingli's understanding of the gospel was maturing, as he wrestled with Paul and John, as well as Augustine, and as he underwent experiences as diverse as the plague and his own failure as a person and a minister.

In his preaching of the gospel Luther attacked works, whereas Zwingli attacked idolatry, that is putting one's trust in anything other than God, which of course included works. (The different emphases are characteristic of other differences in their theology.) Zwingli's concern needs to be set in the context of Zurich, where in the period before the Reformation Farner speaks of an immense increase in images, processions, and pilgrimages.[1]

Two of Zwingli's favourite texts indicate the positive and negative side of idolatry. It is put negatively in the words of Jeremiah, 'They have forsaken me, the fountain of living waters, and have hewn out for themselves cisterns, broken cisterns, that can hold no water' (Jer. 2: 13). It was put positively in the words, 'Come to me, all who labour and are heavy laden, and I will give you rest' (Matt. 11: 28). By contrast we tell people: 'run here, drive there, buy indulgences, paint the walls [with images of saints], give to the monk, offer up to the priest, fatten the nuns, then I—one person to another—will absolve you etc.' Repeating the same word of Christ Zwingli stated, 'Note how he calls us unto himself and does not point us to this one or that one of the advocates'. (Z II 66.13–16, 221.25–7; *Writings* i. 80, 174.)

Pilgrimages, prayer to the saints, even works of mercy and sacraments were or could be idolatrous, for they all made Christ and his death secondary or dispensable. Faith was to be placed not in them but in God.

[1] O. Farner, *Huldrych Zwingli* (Zurich, 1954), iii. 19–20.

The true religion of Christ, then, consists in this: that wretched man despairs of himself, and rests all his thought and confidence on God, sure that he can refuse nothing who has given his Son for us; and that the Son, who is equally God with the Father, can refuse nothing, since he is ours. But false religion merely juggles with the name of Christ, having its hope elsewhere. For, to wash away his sins, one man hires drunken singers, another monks to engage in empty psalmody; one thinks to purchase blessedness by building pretentious churches, another by having costly raiment made for some saint; one rests on his own works, another on those of somebody else.... Almighty God, grant that we may all recognize our blindness, and that we who have thus far clung to creatures may henceforth cleave to the Creator, that he may be our only treasure and our heart abide with him.

After that Zwingli concludes with the words 'So much on the chief and essential point of the Christian religion'. (Z III 723.1–17; *Works* iii. 156.)

The strong emphasis on God in Zwingli's theology is characteristic of his view of salvation which he saw as from God and in God. It begins in God's election and depends entirely on his will and purpose, and not on us. God's election, however, is in Christ, which does not simply mean the eternal Christ, but the Christ who was born, suffered, died, rose, and ascended for the salvation of mankind. Salvation, however, is not accomplished in us, until the Spirit leads us to faith. For Zwingli therefore salvation was seen to be altogether the work of God—Father, Son, and Holy Spirit.

The insistence on God's grace in Christ was common to all the reformers. It led to their denial of free will and merit, and was accompanied by a doctrine of human sinfulness. Zwingli and Luther were at one in their opposition to free will and merit in debate with Erasmus and others, although there were some differences between Zwingli and Luther in their understanding of sin. Indeed Zwingli's attack on free will in *A Commentary* was published before Luther's challenge to Erasmus in *The Bondage of the Will*. Zwingli's attack, like Luther's, was an attack on works which were called good, but were not, either because they did not arise from faith or because they were not commanded by God, as for example pilgrimages. It was also an attack on regarding our works as the basis of our salvation or standing with God. They affirmed that truly good works spring from faith, for a living faith produces good works, as a good tree produces good fruit. In debate with his opponents Zwingli allowed that many passages of scripture ascribe salvation to works and speak of God's rewarding our works. However he followed Augustine in asserting that in such references it is his own work and not ours that God is rewarding, for it is he who effects the good we do. He points out that in the end everything depends on God's election of us before the foundation of the world. (S IV 62.21–44.)

The opening articles at the first disputation show that for Zwingli, as for Luther, Christ is at the heart of the gospel he preached and that his concern like Luther's was a pastoral concern for people's souls.

> The summary of the gospel is, that our Lord Jesus Christ, the true Son of God, has revealed the will of his heavenly Father to us, and with his innocence has redeemed us from death, and has reconciled us with God.
>
> Therefore, Christ is the only way to salvation for all those who have been, are, and will be.
>
> Whoever seeks or points out another door errs, yes, he is a murderer of souls and a thief. (Z I 458.13–19.)

Within Zwingli's summary of the gospel there is a reference to revealing the will of the Father which marks Zwingli off from Luther. It is one of the differences in emphasis and in terminology between Zwingli and Luther; and some of them led to important differences in Lutheran and Reformed theology. From the beginning there was in Zwingli a concern with the living of the new life. This is probably related both to the influence on Zwingli of Erasmian humanism and to his reading of the fathers. In his earliest reformation writing Zwingli spoke of the gospel as firing people with the love of God and neighbour (Z I 88.10–89.2). In his concern for the transformation of people's lives he could even say that it would have been better not to send a redeemer at all than to send one and then for us not to change (Z III 787.20–7).

In this the example of Christ, which was so important in

humanist circles, remained a part of Zwingli's theology as a reformer. When commenting on 'Put on the Lord Jesus Christ' (Rom. 13: 14), he described the life of a Christian as 'nothing other than acknowledging oneself a sinner, trusting in God's mercy through Christ, and building a life in holiness and innocence according to Christ's example' (S VI ii. 126.12–29). Such a life is, however, no longer a matter of human effort, but it is constantly presented as the work of Christ or the Spirit in the Christian. In his stress on the new life of the Christian Zwingli attacked the anabaptists, whom he accused of talking rather than living the life of Christ, and Catholics whom he accused of cutting the Christian life off from its source in Christ.

Zwingli differed from Luther in the way he used certain crucial terms, in particular righteousness and law and gospel. For Luther righteousness was Christ's righteousness imputed to us. For Zwingli it was that, but it was also (and here he is closer to Augustine) Christ's righteousness imparted to us. In his earliest writings Zwingli used the terms law and gospel in a way close to Luther's, but from his letter to Strasbourg in 1524 a different emphasis was present. The order became gospel and law, for he spoke of faith 'as the foundation on which the law is built'. (Z VII 263.18–265.24.) In his early writings Zwingli like Luther spoke of the impossibility of fulfilling the law and of Christ's giving it to us so that we may recognize our shortcomings and take refuge in him. But Zwingli was critical of Luther's negative way of describing the law. The law itself is holy, and one ought not, like Luther, to speak of it as frightening us, bringing us to despair, causing us to hate God. Despair and hatred of God are not an effect of the law, but come from our weakness and our inability to keep the law. As Zwingli was to put it later in a comment on Jas. 1: 25, the law does not condemn any more than light shining on people who are deformed makes them deformed (S VI ii. 260.24–261.23).

Far from opposing the law to the gospel, as Luther did, Zwingli could even speak of the law as gospel. In expounding the sixteenth article in 1523 Zwingli stated that he regarded as gospel 'everything which God has made known to us through his own Son' and that includes a command like 'You shall not be angry with one another.' If you see law from the standpoint of the believer it is in fact gospel or good news. 'The true believer is gladdened and nourished with every word of God, even if it is against the desires of the flesh.' (Z II 231.33–233.15.)

For Zwingli Christ fulfilled the law in two senses: in showing what God wants from us and in doing what we could not do, to satisfy God's righteousness. The law is therefore renewed by Christ by being expressed more clearly. (Z II 496.6–22.) But Christ has freed us from the law 'not so that we are never to do what God commands or wills', but rather so that we should do what God wills out of the love stimulated by God's grace and friendship (Z II 235.4–236.33).

We are free from the law because Christ (or the Spirit) is at work in us doing what the law commands or—and this is not fundamentally different—because those who love do not need the law to tell them what to do. However, as many people's faith is weak, the law is necessary. 'Hence we preach the law as well as grace. For from the law the faithful and elect learn the will of God; and the wicked are also affrighted so that they either serve their neighbour through fear or reveal all their desperation and unbelief.' (S IV 63.31–45; LCC xxiv. 273; *Works* ii. 269.) Here we see the so-called third use of the law, in addition to its restraining of evil and its exposing of human sinfulness.

For Zwingli the civil and ceremonial laws which concern the outward man are not eternal, but only those which concern the inward man. In contrast to his Catholic opponents he regarded the so-called counsels in the gospels as binding on all Christians. They are summed up in Christ or in love, for Christ and love are said to be the end of the law (Rom. 10: 4 and 1 Tim. 1: 5).

Some differences between Zwingli and Luther relate to differences in their understanding of man and of sin. Zwingli argued as strongly as Luther that man is a sinner and in contrast to the Vulgate he translated Gen. 8: 21 as stating that the thoughts of the heart are evil, not that they tend to evil, a translation which had led some to speak of man's free will. He expressed the view of man as a sinner in the Pauline opposition of flesh and spirit. In this the word flesh refers to the whole man and not a part of man, and describes him as fallen. Man therefore can do nothing for his own salvation. In this contrast the Spirit refers to the Holy Spirit. But Zwingli also worked, as Erasmus did, with a Greek opposition of flesh and spirit or body and soul. Although the Pauline view is dominant in Zwingli's view of salvation, the Greek view runs through all his thought. It particularly affected his understanding of the way men and women receive salvation, for it resisted the idea that word and sacrament as outward things could mediate salvation to the heart and soul, which are inward.

Zwingli's initial discussion of sin in *An Exposition of the Articles* was set in the context of salvation. It was after articles two to four which affirmed Christ as saviour, that article five dealt with the nature of sin. Moreover Zwingli described the underlying sickness in order that our healing or salvation could be understood better. He began the discussion with Adam who turned from God to himself, wanting to become like God. He disobeyed God's command and consequently suffered the penalty of death. As a result all his descendants are dead. Without the Spirit of God all people are dead and powerless to do good. Zwingli's discussions of sin are based largely on Genesis, as here, and Romans. From Romans he drew the role of the law as showing us what sin is and as making us despair of coming to God of ourselves.

In *A Commentary* Zwingli stressed that Adam's seeking to be equal with God sprang from self-love. The resulting disease in us as Adam's descendants can be described not only as death and powerlessness, as before, but also as self-love. (Self-love corresponds with concupiscence in Luther.) Zwingli used the traditional distinction between original sin (disease or weakness) and actual sin (or transgression) which flows out of it. Like Augustine and Luther, he affirmed the total corruption of sin.

It was controversy with the anabaptists which led to an important re-expression of his view of sin. In *Baptism, Rebaptism, and Infant Baptism* in May 1525 he emphasized sin as voluntary transgression of the law and distinguished original sin from original guilt. In his debate with anabaptists he was arguing for infant baptism, but could not use the traditional argument that baptism deals with original sin as that was in conflict with his understanding of baptism. He argued that original sin which is inborn in us 'is a defect which of itself is not sinful in the one who has it'. He added: 'it also cannot damn him, whatever the theologians say, until out of this defect he does something against the law of God. But he does not do anything against the law, until he knows the law.' He based his argument on passages like 'where there is no law, there is no transgression' (Rom. 4: 15) and 'The son shall not bear the guilt of the father' (Eze. 18: 20). (Z IV 307.11–312.4, 315.10–25.)

Luther attacked Zwingli's position as Pelagian, regarding him as opening the way for free will. In *Original Sin*, published in 1526, Zwingli spoke of original sin as a disease (*morbus*), though not in the sense of something temporary in contrast to a defect (*vitium*) which lasts. 'I use it as combined with a defect and that a lasting one, as when stammering, blindness, or gout is hereditary in a family.... On account of such a thing no one is thought the worse or the more vicious. For such things which come from nature, cannot be put down as crimes or guilt.' (Z V 370.23–7, 371.11–372.3; *Works* ii. 4–5.) He drew an analogy with being born a slave because one's ancestors had been captured and made slaves.

He gave a varied response to the question whether original sin damns us. We are sinners as we are descendants of a sinner. However if we are sinners, we are enemies of God and therefore damned. But Zwingli qualifies this apparently clear statement by reference to Jacob who was beloved of God before he was born, so that original sin could not have damned him. He supports this with reference to the covenant with Abraham's seed in Gen. 17: 7, which includes the children of Christian parents. 'If, therefore, he promises that he will be a God to Abraham's seed, that seed cannot have been damned because of original guilt'. Besides these arguments which relate to election Zwingli also developed an argument relating to Christ's work as making good the evil done by Adam, a point made in relation to Rom. 5: 19–21. (Z V 380–7; *Works* ii. 20.) Zwingli applied this to the children of Christian parents, but held back from applying it to the whole human race.

Zwingli's mature position was that it is the nature of original sin, taken by itself to damn, for it leads to actual sin. However Christ has made good what Adam did, so that it does not damn those who trust in him or their children. This can be seen in the fourth of the Marburg articles which united him at least verbally with Luther. It held that original sin damns if you consider its nature and if you do not relate it to the work of Christ. The article of course has no reference to Zwingli's distinction between original sin and original guilt nor to his insistence that there is no damnation until there is transgression.

Zwingli affirmed, as Luther and Augustine, man's total corruption and his incapacity to contribute to his own salvation. In this he was opposed to the medieval stress on works and the emphasis of Erasmus and others on free will. Zwingli's sense of the sovereignty and centrality of God affected his whole understanding of salvation, including his understanding of sin. The attack on idolatry focused the attention on trust in God over against everything and everyone other than God. His elaboration of his thinking (in terms of election, faith, and works or love) puts the emphasis on God who elects and on Christ or the Spirit who work in us to lead us to faith and a new life of love.

8

Word and Sacrament

THE word Zwinglian is most often linked with Zwingli's view of the sacraments, usually to imply that whereas Luther was positive and affirmed the real presence of Christ in the Lord's Supper, Zwingli was negative and affirmed the real absence! There are many points where Zwingli spoke positively about word and sacrament. However the hundreds of pages written against his opponents—Catholic, Lutheran, anabaptist—are more taken up with refuting his opponents' positions than with stating his own. He was therefore as much concerned to assert what word and sacrament are not as what they are.

Zwingli attacked the way that word and sacrament had become a source of false confidence, replacing faith in God with faith in the outward word or the outward sacrament. This was, as we have seen, idolatry, for it took away God's honour and gave it to the creature. Salvation, it seemed, could be guaranteed simply by hearing the word, or being baptized, or receiving holy communion. If salvation came from word and sacrament, then repentance and faith were unnecessary.

Zwingli's stress on the sovereignty of God, which in fact underlies the whole of his theology, is most evident in his understanding of word and sacrament. He rejected any idea that they could be effective in or of themselves, for such a view denied the sovereignty of God. If God were bound by word and sacrament, then salvation would be put at man's disposal. We could do (or have done to us) something which guarantees our salvation. Zwingli had many objections to this view; fundamental among them was that salvation depended utterly on God, not on word and sacrament, even though they are given by God. But God is not bound to them in the sense that he must act through them and cannot act apart from them, for that would limit the sovereign freedom of the Spirit who blows where he wills. He maintained this position consistently against Catholic and Lutheran opponents.

His difference from Luther can be seen in the texts which each of them emphasized when speaking of the word. For Luther it was texts such as 'So faith comes from what is heard, and what is heard comes from the preaching of Christ' (Rom. 10: 17) and 'So shall my word be that goes forth from my mouth; it shall not return to me empty, but it shall accomplish that which I purpose' (Isa. 55: 11).

For Zwingli besides Johannine texts such as 'No one can come to me unless the Father who sent me draws him' (John 6: 44), 'And they shall all be taught of God' (John 6: 45), and 'The Spirit blows where he wills' (John 3: 8), there was the text which he never tired of quoting against Luther: 'It is the Spirit who gives life, the flesh is of no avail' (John 6: 63). There was also the Pauline word: 'I planted, Apollos watered, but God gave the growth. So neither he who plants nor he who waters is anything, but only God who gives the growth' (1 Cor. 3: 6–7).

The stress on God's sovereignty does not mean that preaching is unnecessary or unimportant. For Zwingli preaching was central to his reforming ministry in Zurich, and it was through preaching that the city was being changed. But the Spirit came from God, not from the preaching. Thus in 1522 when he reviewed the preaching he had done since his arrival in Zurich at the end of 1518 he could say, 'This is the seed I have sown, Matthew, Luke, Paul, and Peter have watered it, and God has given it splendid increase.' (Z I 285.25–7; *Works* i. 239.)

Zwingli did on occasion speak of the word as if it was automatically effective. When however he spoke of the power of the word, it was not in terms of anything in the word but in terms of God's doing all things according to his sovereign will. 'The Word of God is so sure and strong that if God wills all things are done the moment that he speaks his Word.' (Z I 353.8–9; LCC xxiv. 68.)

Zwingli's view of the word was rooted in scripture and experience. They were both evidence of the fact that the word is not automatically effective, for many then, as now, did not believe. But scripture also testifies that God chose men to minister and that he has used human ministry to lead people to faith. For Zwingli the word was indispensable in the offer of salvation as in the reformation of the church. He expressed this positive view in *An Account of the Faith*. 'For in speaking canonically or regularly we see that among all nations the outward preaching of apostles and evangelists or bishops has preceded faith, which we nevertheless say is received by the Spirit alone.' (Z VI ii. 813.8–11; Jackson 478; *Works* ii. 56.) The sending of a preacher is a sign of God's grace because God always sends a prophet to prepare the way of the Lord, even though he could simply enlighten people's hearts by the Spirit (S VI i. 550.8–22). It was because of the importance of the word that Zwingli made the preaching of the gospel a condition of peace with the Catholic cantons in 1529.

Here, as in other areas, Zwingli made a distinction between what God could have done and what he actually did. He could have saved people without the word and without human instruments, but he chose to use them, as he chose to use herbs for healing. The main reason he gave for God's use of preachers to preach the word is that God has made people with senses and in need of admonition, unlike angels who see him continually. (S VI i. 582.19–32.) The preacher and the word are, however, not causes but only instruments, as in their different ways water, fire, and the sun are also only instruments. It is God who is the true cause of everything, including the warmth of the fire or the sun (Z VI iii. 112.18–24; *Works* ii. 156).

Despite the positive way Zwingli could speak of the word and the agreement reached between Zwingli and Luther at Marburg, there was a fundamental difference between them. The eighth of the Marburg articles was written by Luther, but he expressed the article in such a way that Zwingli could sign it as well as Luther. It stated what was of greatest importance for him: that it is the Spirit, and not the outward word, who gives faith.

For Luther, it was through the word that we receive the Spirit and faith so that he could write 'through the word, which is the door and window of the Holy Spirit. . . . He will use that door, which is the word whether written or spoken.' (*WA* 20. 451.7–10.) For Zwingli, however, a 'channel or vehicle is not necessary to the Spirit, for he himself is the virtue and energy whereby all things are borne and has no need of being borne' (Z VI ii. 803.10–12; *Works* ii. 46). There is the same underlying difference in their approach to the sacraments, a difference that is rooted in their differing understandings of the sovereignty of God and in other differences of doctrine, but also in Zwingli's Platonism. Zwingli stressed God's sovereignty over word and sacrament, while Luther stressed God's sovereignty in them. For Zwingli the creature was set over against God as leading us from God into idolatry, for Luther the creature was rather a mask for God through which God comes to us. But there was also Zwingli's Platonism. For him nothing outward, as word and sacrament are, could affect what is inward.

The differences between Zwingli and his opponents (Catholic, Lutheran, and anabaptist) were more evident in the sacraments than in the word. Moreover as Zwingli's writings are an attack on their views, his position often appears in a negative rather than a positive form. Nevertheless, even in 1536 when Bucer was regarded by many as Lutheran, he spoke positively of Zwingli's position.

> Christ alone effects the whole of salvation in us, and he does it not by some other power, but by his Spirit alone. However, for this he uses with us the word, both the visible word in the sacraments and the audible word in the gospel. By them he brings and offers remission of sins.... Zwingli recognized that; hence, when he denied that the sacraments dispense grace, he meant that the sacraments, that is the outward action, are not of themselves effective, but that everything belonging to our salvation depends on the inward action of Christ, of whom the sacraments are, in their way, instruments.[1]

Zwingli's views were stated initially against Catholic opponents. Already in *An Exposition of the Articles* in 1523, he was particularly troubled by the use of the term sacrament. He had several objections. It was a Latin term which was misunderstood by Germans; it was a word not used by Christ;

[1] *In sacra quatuor evangelia, Enarrationes perpetuae* (Basle, 1536), 485 B.

and it grouped together rites that are better understood in terms of their own individual names. Like Erasmus he pointed out that sacrament comes from *sacramentum* meaning an oath. For this reason it could be used of things which 'God has instituted, commanded, and ordained with his word, which is as firm and sure as if he had sworn an oath thereto' (Z II 120.25–8). On this basis Zwingli rejected as sacraments rites, such as confirmation, which God had not ordained.

In 1524 there was an important shift as Zwingli began to use the term oath as our oath or pledge rather than as God's oath. In a discussion of 1 Cor. 10: 16–17 the sacrament was seen as 'an inward and outward union of Christian people'. In it we eat and drink 'so that we may testify to all men that we are one body and one brotherhood'. (Z III 124.32–3, 125.10–14.) The accent shifted from God to Christians as the subject of the sacraments.

The shift of accent from God to man coincides with a movement away from seeing the sacraments as an assurance of forgiveness and a strengthening of faith. In a letter to Fridolin Lindauer in October 1524 the sacraments are said to be given to instruct the outward man which grasps things through the senses. Thus God satisfies the whole man, inward and outward, by commanding that the person who already believes inwardly should be baptized outwardly. (Z VIII 236.3–13.) As Zwingli put it in December 1524, 'our eyes want also to see, otherwise Christ would not have instituted baptism and the eucharistic bread' (Z III 411.16–18).

The understanding of the sacraments as an oath or pledge was the basis from which Zwingli attacked other views (especially Catholic and Lutheran, but also anabaptist) in *A Commentary*. A sacrament 'cannot have any power to free the conscience, if it is simply an initiation or public inauguration'. Only God is able to free the conscience. (Z III 759.18–21.) He rejected the view that what was done outwardly was also done inwardly, by examples from the New Testament as well as by reference to the freedom of the Spirit. He offered a different understanding of sacraments. They are 'signs by which a man proves to the church that he either aims to be, or is, a soldier of Christ, and which inform the whole church rather than yourself of your faith'. (Z III 761.22–38; *Works* iii. 184.)

In 1525 there was an important change in Zwingli's view of sacraments as signs of the covenant, deriving from his changed understanding of the covenant. He had naturally used the term covenant of God's covenant with man, but in 1525 this view was developed and related to the sacraments as signs of the covenant of grace made by God with man, that he will be their God, and they will be his people. This enabled Zwingli to move from the earlier view of sacraments as a covenant or pledge between Christians. Although this development took place in terms of the eucharist, it was particularly important in his controversy with the anabaptists, as it gave greater coherence to his arguments for infant baptism.

Zwingli accepted the traditional definition of Augustine and Peter Lombard that a sacrament is 'the sign of a holy thing'. However he made a sharp distinction between the sign and what it signifies. Signs cannot be what they signify, or they are no longer signs. For him a sacrament does not make present what it signifies, but it shows and attests that what it signifies is there. It is the sign, as he later put it, not of a grace that is given, but of one that has been given (Z VI ii. 805.6–7). Zwingli's view of signs is related to his understanding of the sovereignty of God, but also to a Platonist opposition between the outward and the inward.

In Zwingli's later writings in 1530 and 1531 his views are presented more positively, in part through the mediating influence of Bucer and others and the attempts at reconciliation leading to the Marburg Colloquy in 1529; but the changes are ones of emphasis rather than of substance. The stress on the sovereignty of God remains, with the insistence that the Spirit does not need outward means and is certainly not bound by them, either in the sense that he must work where they are present, for 'if it were thus it would be known how, where, whence and whither the Spirit is borne', or in the sense that he cannot work apart from them, for the Spirit blows where he wills. However the freedom of the Spirit in relation to the sacraments is also expressed more positively. 'And one and the same Spirit works all these things, sometimes without, sometimes with, the external instrument, and in inspiring draws where, as much, and whom he wills.' (Z VI ii. 803.22–804.25; *Works* ii. 46; Z VI iii. 271.10–12; *Works* ii. 117.)

The term sacramentarian was one used by Luther and others to characterize Zwingli's position on the sacraments. Zwingli however used it in reply to describe those who 'attribute to the symbols what belongs only to the divine power and the Holy Spirit working immediately in our souls', and who thus lead people away from simple trust in God to trust in the power of symbols. His concern is that glory shall be given to God and not to the sacraments. (Z VI iii. 173.4–5; *Works* ii. 194; Z VI iii. 270.18–21.) This concern and its suspicion of outward things must be related not only to Zwingli's stress on the sovereignty of God and his Platonism, but also to the state of medieval religion, with its superstitious attachment to people, places, and things, and not least to the sacraments, and with the financial exploitation of this by the church. This attachment was for Zwingli quite simply a restoration of Judaism (Z VI ii. 805.23–9).

As the Bible is full of examples of God's making use of what is outward to accomplish his purposes, Zwingli's biblical commentaries naturally refer to this. They accept that God used outward means, though he could have acted without them. Nevertheless the power is God's and does not dwell in the means.

> And to put it briefly, the ground does not bring forth, nor the water nourish, nor the air fructify, nor the fire warm, nor the sun itself, but rather that power which is the origin of all things, their life and strength, uses the earth as the instrument wherewith to produce and create (Z VI iii. 112.20–4; *Works* ii. 156).

This sense that God is at work in all things might have led to a more positive view of the sacraments. Such a view could have safeguarded God's sovereignty, and Zwingli could have used the doctrine of election, as Bucer did, to indicate that the sacraments are effective only with the elect. Like him he could have expressed the distinction between outward and inward by using the preposition 'with' (rather than Luther's other prepositions 'in' and 'under') to express the relationship between the sign and what is signified. However the strong opposition between outward and inward in Zwingli probably prevented this development, although his last major work *An Exposition of the Faith* offers an essentially positive presentation of the sacraments.

Under the heading 'The Power (or Virtue) of the Sacraments', Zwingli lists seven powers or virtues of the sacraments. First, they are instituted by Christ who received the one and celebrated the other. Secondly, they testify to actual historical events. Thirdly, they take the place and name of what they signify. Fourthly, they signify high things, where the analogy is used of the queen's ring, the value of which comes less from the gold than from the value of the king it represents. (As Zwingli put it elsewhere 'it so represents him who so loves us that we gaze upon him with the eye of the mind and adore and worship him'.) Fifthly, there is a twofold analogy: bread sustains human life as Christ sustains the soul, and bread is made up of many grains as the body of the church is made up of many members. The sixth virtue is expounded at greatest length and states that the sacraments 'augment faith and are an aid to it'. This comes through their powerful appeal to the senses. When the senses would lead us astray, they check them and 'recall them to the obedience of the heart and of faith', so that they 'assist the contemplation of faith'. The seventh virtue is that they act as an oath with which we are joined in one body. (S IV 58.18–60.27; LCC xxiv. 263–4; *Works* ii. 258–9.)

This last virtue demonstrates the way in which throughout his writings Zwingli links the sacraments to the church. He understands them corporately in terms of the church rather than individually in terms of salvation. This is expressed in the two ways in which they were covenant signs: as our pledge to our fellow believers that we are one with them in God's people, and as God's pledge to us that he is our God and that we are his people.

Although there is a fundamental continuity, there are also changes in Zwingli's view of the sacraments. At first the sacraments are signs of the covenant with which God assures us; then they are signs with which we assure others that we are one with them in the church; finally both these elements are present. Again, at the beginning the sacraments are said to strengthen faith; later this view is rejected; but at the end it is present in a modified form, in that through their appeal to the senses the sacraments can be said to strengthen faith, though there is no sense in which they can give faith. Nevertheless the role of the senses is not new in the later Zwingli, even if it is expressed more positively there than it was earlier. However nothing for Zwingli can take from the sovereignty of God who alone gives faith and who, although he may use outward means, has no need of them.

9

Baptism

FROM the beginning there were those in Zurich who were more radical than Zwingli in wanting to move faster and further in reformation of the church than he did. The differences between them concerned social matters (such as tithes and interest, the role of government, and the use of the oath) as well as religious matters (such as images and baptism).

In some cases, at least on the surface, their differences had to do with the right moment or the right method. That was true when some broke the fast by eating meat in Lent in 1522. Zwingli was present, but although he agreed with them and later defended them he did not join them. It was also true in the summer of 1523 when opposition to images led some radicals to smash images in churches. Again Zwingli agreed with their view, but he did not join in their action. Moreover in the disputation in October 1523 which held images and the mass to be unscriptural, although both he and they agreed on their abolition, Zwingli again proved more cautious and was prepared to leave the timing of the action to the council.

There were, however, differences of substance, hidden sometimes in matters of method and timing, but manifest in divergent understandings of baptism and the church. Other differences were also evident in the representations about tithes and interest in July 1523, where the radicals had a vision of society based on the Sermon on the Mount. Zwingli recognized the force of their appeal to what he called divine righteousness, but he argued that human society must be based on human rather than divine righteousness. Their different understanding of the church emerged in October 1523 when Zwingli was prepared to leave the timing of change to the council, whereas they thought that the council had no place at all in the life of the church. Their differences came into even sharper focus in 1524 and 1525 over the question of baptism. They rejected infant baptism in favour of believers' baptism and claimed that Zwingli had once agreed with them. At first they simply declined to have their children baptized, but then in January 1525 they began to rebaptize those who had been baptized as children. It was after this that Zwingli wrote his four main works about baptism, although his views on baptism were as much opposed to those of Catholics and Lutherans as to those of the anabaptists.

Before the baptismal controversy Zwingli said little about baptism and in what he wrote the emphasis was on faith rather than baptism. He believed that baptism could strengthen faith, but denied that it could give faith. In *An Exposition of the Articles* in July 1523 he appeared to accept infant baptism, and his concern was that those baptized as infants should be properly instructed in the faith and that they should not be confirmed until they were able to confess the faith. Looking back later, however, he admitted that there had been a time when he thought it much better not to baptize children until they had come to years of discretion (Z IV 228.20–229.7). This was because he had held that baptism strengthened faith, which it could not do with infants who cannot have faith.

It was in 1524 that some people raised more openly questions about baptism. As early as February that year a number refused to have their children baptized, and in the autumn Manz and Grebel were in touch with Müntzer and welcomed his criticism of infant baptism. Zwingli had abortive discussions with some of the radicals in December, and in the same month set out his position in a letter to Strasbourg (Z VIII 261–78). He stated that in the Bible 'baptism is the initiation both of those who have already believed and those who are going to believe'. In it baptism preceded knowledge of Christ and was given so that people 'might learn Christ afterwards'. Secondly, he argued for infant baptism on the grounds that it replaced circumcision (Col. 2: 11) which was given to infants, although it was a sign of prior faith (Rom. 4: 11). Thirdly, he drew on the words of

Christ in Matt. 19: 13–14, saying that if anyone forbids children to be baptized, he forbids them to come to Christ.

Zwingli also dealt with a number of the objections to infant baptism raised by his opponents. In dealing with the objections that there are no statements or examples in the New Testament in support of infant baptism, Zwingli argued that it is more likely than not that there were children in the households baptized in 1 Cor. 1 and Acts 16. In response to two challenges about faith preceding baptism in Mark 16: 16 and about the apostles' examining beforehand the faith of those they baptized, he argued first that Mark 16: 16, as the previous verse shows, applies only to adults to whom the gospel is preached and not to infants, and secondly, that the apostles only sometimes examined people beforehand.

In another treatise at the same time he dealt again with the fact that the New Testament gives no command about baptizing infants and no example of it. He allows that there is no command, but adds that there is also no prohibition. He argues that the fact that the apostles did not baptize infants does not mean that we should not, any more than the fact that they did not baptize in Calcutta means that we should not baptize in Calcutta. Moreover since the New Testament gives no clear guidance we should turn to the Old Testament and that gives us circumcision which was administered to infants. The appeal to the Old Testament was alien to the radicals, and Zwingli had later to argue his case for appealing to it for support. He did this in part in terms of Christ's appealing to the Old Testament.

The crisis with the radicals came to a head in January 1525 when the council summoned the radicals and Zwingli, along with the other ministers, to a disputation on 17 January. After it the council insisted on the baptism of infants within eight days, on pain of banishment. However on 21 January Grebel baptized Blaurock, who then baptized fifteen others. A day or two later he presided at an evangelical celebration of the Lord's Supper in a house in Zollikon. Despite official action against it the movement spread to other cantons and beyond. Further meetings or disputations between the reformers and the radicals in March and November produced no change, and on 7 March

1526 the council declared that anyone rebaptizing would be put to death by drowning. The first to suffer in this way was Felix Manz on 5 January 1527.

The debate with the radicals forced Zwingli to differentiate his position from theirs, though they shared in part his view of the sacraments. For him their insistence on believers' baptism called in question salvation through Christ alone, as in their different ways Catholic and Lutheran understandings of baptism also did. In the course of the debate Zwingli elaborated his earlier views on baptism, but there was a major development (in his understanding of covernant) which gave greater coherence to his view of baptism whether administered to adults or to children.

A typical example of the anabaptist case for believers' baptism can be found in a treatise from this period, probably written by Grebel or Manz who had joined the radicals in the summer of 1522. It regarded infant baptism as a popish invention and stated both that Christ did not teach and that the apostles did not practise infant baptism. Moreover Christ commanded those who had been taught to be baptized, while the apostles baptized only those who had been taught and who desired baptism. Christ is presented as an example to us, for he was baptized at the age of 30, but circumcised when eight days old. Furthermore, it was argued, baptism is for those seeking to lead a new life. (Z III 368–372.) The need to have faith and the desire for a new life was seen as clear evidence that only adults could be baptized. Some anabaptists, such as Hubmaier, held very moderate views. Thus in a letter to Oecolampadius he wrote that he would baptize children where the parents were weak and insisted on it (S II i. 339.4–11).

Zwingli's first response to the rebaptism in January 1525 came in *A Commentary*. In it he argued for the identity of John's baptism and Christ's baptism. He did this to demonstrate that there was no need for as well as no case of a second baptism in Acts 19, a chapter used by the anabaptists in support of rebaptism. He dealt also in general with the meaning of sacraments, describing them as signs 'by which a man proves to the church that he either aims to be, or is, a soldier of Christ, and which inform the whole church rather than yourself of your faith'. Baptism is an initiatory ceremony or pledging and not, as anabaptists claimed, a sign which makes a person sure of what has been done within him. Furthermore it does not as Catholics asserted free or cleanse the conscience, nor as Lutherans held does it make a person sure that the Spirit does inwardly what the sacrament signifies outwardly. (Z III 757–762; *Works* iii. 184.)

The conflict intensified after this and Zwingli published three major works against the anabaptists—two in 1525 *Baptism, Rebaptism, and Infant Baptism* and *A Reply to Hubmaier* and one in 1527 *A Refutation*. Finally, in 1530, there was a reply to questions about baptism raised by Schwenckfeld. Zwingli's concern was not with the issue of baptism only, but with the threat posed to the Reformation itself by the radical approach of the anabaptists on baptism and social issues. (He had already dealt with some of these. Thus he used the command not to steal to defend personal property against the radicals' attack on private ownership.) He criticized their divisiveness in separating from the church to set up their own sinless churches.

The main lines of Zwingli's defence of infant baptism remained the same as in the letter to Strasbourg: what happened in the course of the controversy is that he refined his position and added important supporting arguments. Although infant baptism was the main issue, the discussion of it was set in the context of a general discussion of baptism.

For him both Catholics and anabaptists were guilty of overemphasizing outward baptism, for 'no outward element or action can purify the soul' (Z IV 252.21–6). Christ did away with outward things, so that we should not seek our salvation in them. It was a concession to our weakness that he gave us baptism, but he gave it as a pledge, a sign of a sacred thing, and not the sacred thing itself. (Z IV 216.26–217.23.) Baptism is an initiatory sign, like the cowl a man has on entering an order, which he wears before learning the rules of the order. Zwingli used Matt. 28: 19–20, a favourite anabaptist text, as a support for his case because in it baptism precedes the teaching of what the baptized are to observe. (Z IV 231.26–30, 231.32–233.16.)

This view of baptism as an initiatory sign or pledge could be applied to infant as well as adult baptism. Zwingli held that baptism should be given to infants as they are part of God's people, for the children of Christian parents are no less children of God than their parents are, just as much as was the case in the Old Testament. If they are God's, who will refuse them baptism? (Z IV 333.24–6.) If they are not baptized, then we would have a part of God's people baptized and a part not baptized (Z IV 318.3–12). Moreover they should receive baptism as children because baptism replaces circumcision which was given to children.

Besides this essentially positive point, Zwingli had to deal with the range of arguments against infant baptism. He advanced some additional arguments, although the one which continued to be presented at greatest length was the identity of John's baptism and Christ's baptism. He rejected the view that children cannot have the Spirit. Among other examples he pointed out that while still in his mother's womb John the Baptist acknowledged Christ with greater joy than we who are adults. God works how and when he will, regardless of age. (Z IV 242.10–27.)

Zwingli did not deny the anabaptist assertion that Christ did not baptize infants, but he challenged the conclusion that we should therefore not baptize infants, arguing that otherwise by implication women should not come to holy communion, as there were no women at the Last Supper (Z IV 296.1–7). (In any case one should beware of saying that something did not happen because it was not recorded as happening, as after all there is no record that most of the apostles were baptized.) He met their assertion that since 'God does not command the baptism of infants, therefore we should not baptize them' with the rebuke that they are guilty of that of which they accuse others: adding to the word of God by prohibiting what God does not prohibit (Z IV 301.31–302.4, 211.8–212.4).

Zwingli drew, moreover, on 1 Cor. 10:1–5 as an argument for the baptism of adults and children, for the passage says that they were all baptized into Moses (Z IV 304.28–306.10). He argued also that the gospel account of children being brought to Jesus favoured infant baptism, for how else can children come to Jesus now, apart from the covenant sign of God's people? And if they belong to God's people, why should one withhold from them the sign of God's people? (Z IV 299.8–300.4.)

A development elsewhere in Zwingli's theology in 1525 produced an important change in his understanding of baptism. It was used at length in a reply to Hubmaier. The covenant is seen as God's covenant of grace, rather than our covenant, his promise rather than ours. The covenant sign, therefore, is the sign of God's covenant and promise, rather than our pledge to live a godly life. This understanding of the sign suited both adult and infant baptism, whereas the earlier understanding of it as a pledge was less coherent, for it meant pledging oneself in the case of adult baptism and pledging to bring up one's children in the case of infant baptism. Moreover, Zwingli argues, the covenant in the New Testament is not a new or different one, but 'we are one in the covenant that God made with Abraham' (Z IV 596.1–2, 636.24–6, 636.33–637.1). The argument was not therefore, as before, in terms of the contrast between the two testaments, so that if something applied to those under the law, how much more does it apply to us under grace. Now it was rather in terms of the unity of the two, for the point of reference is not Moses and the law but the covenant of grace with Abraham.

In *A Refutation* in 1527 he pointed out that the covenant was in fact with Adam in the first instance. There is only one covenant as there is only one God, and he is 'as much our God as he was Abraham's, and we are as much his people as was Israel'. From this it follows that as the children of the Hebrews were one with their parents in the covenant and received the sign of the covenant, so should the children of Christians receive the sign of the covenant, that is baptism, as they are counted in the church of Christ. (Z VI i. 170.12–16, 171.15–19, 171.28–172, 5; *Selected Works* 236.)

Zwingli now also used the argument from election which was in fact used initially against him by the anabaptists. They argued from the rejection of Esau in Rom. 9: 11–13 that infants were not of God's people. Zwingli's reply was that only those whom

God has elected are members of his people, and they are members even if as yet, like infants, they do not believe. The children of Christians are moreover in the covenant as the children of the Hebrews were. This makes us sure of their election until God pronounces differently about them, as he did in the case of Esau. (Z VI i. 175.21–179.19, 184.2–4.)

Zwingli continued to argue from election in his last substantial treatment of baptism, *Questions Concerning the Sacrament of Baptism* (1530), which was a response to forty-six questions raised by Schwenckfeld about baptism. But he used it as a weapon against the anabaptist linking of baptism and faith in support of believers' baptism rather than as the basis of his own case for infant baptism. Among many points two can be taken. First, as we cannot know who are elect and who are reprobate it is wrong to drive from the church the children of Christians to whom God's promise belongs. Secondly, if only those who have faith should be baptized, then nobody can be baptized, for we cannot know for certain about other people's faith. (S III 572–6.)

There were fundamental elements in Zwingli's theology which made him deny the traditional view that baptism is a means of grace and that it is necessary to salvation. For him the traditional view called in question the sovereignty of God, the centrality of Christ, and the freedom of the Spirit. It was also in conflict with the clear witness of scripture that some were baptized who were not saved and some were saved who were not baptized. His view of baptism was bound up with his understanding of salvation, and with his understanding of man, which would not allow that the soul could be affected by what is bodily.

Baptism therefore had a different meaning and purpose for Zwingli from those traditionally given to it. Zwingli saw it as an initiatory sign, a sign of the covenant. This he developed in terms of our pledge to live the Christian life. However as a child could not make a pledge, the pledge made in infant baptism was the parents' pledging of the child and the child's being pledged to the law. In 1525, however, his deepened understanding of the covenant as God's covenant of grace gave him an understanding of covenant signs where the emphasis shifted to God and the church and where the term could be used in fundamentally the same sense for adults and for infants.

In his debate with anabaptists Zwingli relied on two major propositions for the baptism of infants: that children belong to God and should therefore be baptized and that baptism replaces circumcision. They were buttressed by a host of supporting arguments. The most notable development in Zwingli's position came with the changed view of the covenant. This meant that he no longer argued in terms of the contrast between the Old and New Testament but in terms of the unity. Later Zwingli made use of the doctrine of election which had been used first by his opponents. However he used it negatively to undermine their case rather than positively, as Bucer did, as a basis for affirming the effectiveness of baptism with those who are elect, while continuing to assert the sovereignty of God.

10

The Eucharist

THE term Zwinglian is most often used to describe a certain view of the Lord's Supper or eucharist, the subject about which there was the most vigorous and bitter controversy among the reformers. The view is associated with a stress on the eucharist as a memorial. This is often understood or misunderstood as Zwingli's denying the presence of Christ in the eucharist, as if others believed in the real presence and Zwingli in the real absence. Of course Zwingli believed in the presence of Christ, but not his bodily presence, nor his presence in his human nature.

The Early Zwingli: The Sacrifice of Christ and the Presence of Christ

The eucharist was at the centre of medieval religion, and it is natural that it became the focus of the controversy both between the reformers and the medieval church and then among the reformers themselves. In *The Babylonian Captivity of the Church* Luther attacked three ways in which the sacrament had been taken captive: communion in one kind (that is, that lay people received the bread but not the wine), the sacrifice of the mass (the offering of the mass as a sacrifice for the living and the dead), and transubstantiation. On the first two of these, Zwingli and the other reformers were in fundamental agreement with Luther. They appealed to the New Testament to support communion in both kinds (bread and wine) and to assert the sufficiency and unrepeatability of the sacrifice of Christ on the cross. The eucharist does not repeat that sacrifice but is a commemoration of the once for all sacrifice of Christ. It is not something we offer God, but something which he offers to us.

These two points of disagreement between the reformers and the medieval church were frequently expressed in debate between Zwingli and his Catholic opponents and there was no fundamental change in his views. Like Luther he was opposed to the way that masses could be bought, becoming thereby a source of greed and wealth, as well as diverting money from the needs of the poor; but much more important for both of them was the fact that this view of the sacrament imperilled people's salvation, encouraging them to trust in something other than God. Zwingli based his case largely on the Epistle to the Hebrews, but drew also on the fathers as evidence of a view of the eucharist as a commemoration of Christ's sacrifice and not the sacrifice itself.

He addressed the question at the first disputation in January 1523. In the eighteenth article he asserted, 'That Christ, having sacrificed himself once, is to eternity a certain and valid sacrifice for the sins of all faithful, wherefrom it follows that the mass is not a sacrifice, but is a remembrance of the sacrifice and assurance of salvation which Christ has given us.' (Z I 460.6–10; *Selected Works* 112.) In the detailed exposition of this in July 1523 he argued from the priesthood and sacrifice of Christ in Hebrews and claimed that for some years he had called the sacrament 'a memorial of the suffering of Christ and not a sacrifice'. He held that Christ's intention was clear by his saying 'Do this in remembrance of me' and not 'Offer this up to me'. (Z II 137–8.) He also noted a difference in the terms used by himself and Luther. Luther referred to the sacrament as a testament. Zwingli also used that term, but he preferred the term memorial. It is interesting that already at this stage Zwingli's preference was for the more subjective term, for remembering is primarily something which we do rather than something which God does.

Zwingli's position was developed in *The Canon of the Mass* where he defended the term eucharist, although it was not used by Christ or the apostles, as it makes it clear that the sacrament is a gift of God, whereas the term mass makes it something we offer to God (Z II 568.34–569.10). Unlike Grebel, Zwingli allowed liberty to the congregations in what is not clearly prescribed by scripture and did not regard them as bound by the custom of Christ and the apostles in outward matters like time and dress. For the sake of the weak or to avoid divisions he was prepared to use the old forms and formulations.

At this stage Zwingli was conservative in his proposals for reforming the mass and was criticized, for example, for tolerating eucharistic vestments. At the second disputation in the autumn he still did not seek to abolish them, as that would cause an uproar, although he regarded them as a hindrance. He believed that people needed first to be taught. (Z II 788.31–789.16.)

The decision at the second disputation was that the mass was unscriptural and should be abolished. That decision was not, however, put into effect until Easter 1525, as the conservative opposition in Zurich was too strong for the council to move at once. The radicals anticipated this reform by only a few months with their evangelical celebration of the Lord's Supper in the January. The debate with Catholic opponents, such as Joachim am Grüt and Eck, continued, but the major concern moved from the sacrifice of the mass to the presence of Christ in the sacrament.

Christ's presence in the eucharist, as his sacrifice, was also discussed in the first disputation in 1523. At this stage Zwingli's challenge was to the medieval doctrine of transubstantiation—in other words, that the substance of the bread and wine becomes the substance of the body and blood of Christ, while the accidents, that is what the senses apprehend (such as colour and taste) remain those of bread and wine. He rejected this doctrine as an invention of theologians. Although Zwingli referred to the bread and wine as the body and blood of Christ, it is not clear in what sense he regarded the eucharistic elements as the body and blood of Christ. The stress was on the body and blood of Christ as slain for us. He presented his view by expounding John 6 placing the emphasis on faith and on the soul being fed. (He uses the text which was later to be so important: 'It is the Spirit who gives life, the flesh is of no avail' (John 6: 63).) He held that if we believe that 'Christ's body slain for us and his blood shed for us have redeemed us and reconciled us to God

... then our soul receives food and drink with the body and blood of Christ'. With faith the food strengthens us; but without it we eat to our damnation. (Z II 141.14–144.16.) This view that the sacrament strengthens faith was rejected by Zwingli later.

In July 1523 Zwingli wrote to his former teacher, Thomas Wyttenbach, in response to his enquiries about the eucharist. The main concern here, unlike that of the articles, was with the presence of Christ rather than with sacrifice. There is the same emphasis on faith, and faith is related to 'the body of Christ slain for us' for our salvation and not to the eucharistic elements, a factor that was to be important later in his controversy with Luther. The bread and wine can be called the body and blood of Christ, but only 'catachrestically'. They are given to be eaten (not to be reserved or adored) and the stress is on the first half of Christ's word at the Last Supper: 'Take eat' rather than the second half 'This is my body'. There is a shift from the elements to the action. In discussing the presence of Christ, Zwingli used the analogy of a flint to illuminate his understanding of Christ's presence. As there is fire in the flint only when it is struck, so Christ is found under the form of bread and wine only when he is sought in faith. (Z VIII 84–9.)

Scholars differ in their view of how Zwingli understood Christ's presence in the eucharist in 1523 (and before), some arguing for a real or at least a mystical presence, others for a spiritual presence or a presence dependent in some sense on faith, a position compatible with a symbolic view of the sacrament. There are pointers to both views of the sacrament. Yet it should be noted that, although Zwingli used traditional terms, which might seem to imply the former view, they were clearly qualified by other expressions. For example, he referred to the body and blood of Christ but spoke of them as food for the believing soul (Z II 812.7–8). Moreover he allowed those not strong enough to give up an objectionable term like sacrifice to go on using it and yet to understand it as a commemoration of Christ's sacrifice. However from 1524 he clearly held a symbolic view in which the word 'is' in 'This is my body' was interpreted as 'signifies'.

The Symbolic View of the Sacrament

It was in 1524 that Zwingli read the letter by Cornelis Hoen, which Luther had already rejected and which argued for interpreting the word 'is' as 'signifies' in 'This is my body'. Hoen used in support a range of biblical examples including the seven cows and seven ears in Gen. 41 as signifying seven years and the 'I am' passages in St John. Zwingli said that Hoen had helped him to see that the trope was in the word 'is' and not, for example, in the word 'body'.

The impact of Hoen's letter is seen first in a letter of Zwingli to Matthew Alber in November 1524. It is significant, however, that Zwingli dealt with this new insight only in the second part of his letter. In the first part (Z III 336.19–342.10) he concentrated on John 6 which began to have a dominant part in his teaching on the eucharist. (Its importance was to be reflected in its becoming the invariable gospel at holy communion, whereas in the medieval church it had been one of the readings for Corpus Christi.) He recognized that it is not concerned with the eucharist, but for him it disproves certain views of the eucharist, and therefore it is his first line of attack. From it Zwingli shows that it is the flesh of Christ as slain for us and not as eaten by us that is food for the soul. For, as he argued, John 3: 6 makes it clear that what is born of the flesh is flesh, just as what is born of the Spirit is Spirit. Eating the flesh of Christ cannot therefore give birth to anything but flesh. In fact the phrase eating Christ in John 6 means believing in him. Eating his body means believing that he was slain for us. In the whole exposition the two fundamental elements are: the flesh is of no avail and eating is believing.

In the second part (Z III 342.11–347.12) he dealt with what he regarded as the most difficult point: that the words of consecration seem to imply that the bread given by Christ was his body slain for us on the cross. He discounts this on the ground that faith teaches that salvation comes through believing that Christ died for us and not through the sacramental eating of bread and wine. Consequently he holds that there must be a figure of speech in Christ's words. He rejects Carlstadt's view that the word 'this' in 'This is my body' refers to Christ's body rather than the bread, and following Hoen he sees the clue in the word 'is', which is to be understood as 'signifies' just as in many other biblical passages. Furthermore he points to the link between signifying and remembering by noting that 'Take, eat; this is my body' is followed by 'Do this in remembrance of me'. He draws on Tertullian, Augustine, and Origen in support of the term 'signify', referring to Tertullian's use of the term 'represent' and Augustine's use of the term 'figure'. The bread represents Christ's body in that when it is eaten, it calls to remembrance that Christ gave his body for us.

Zwingli also interpreted another key passage (1 Cor. 10: 14–22) used by those who supported bodily eating to support his position. He argued in the light of the following verse ('we who are many are one bread and one body') that 'the communion of the body of Christ' must mean that those who believe testify by eating the bread, that they are members of the same body. What is fundamental therefore is not the eating, but faith, so that we become one body as soon as we believe in Christ. (Z III 347.13–352.3.)

Most of what Zwingli had to say about the eucharist was present, at least implicitly, in his writings by the end of 1524. With each new work some new point or detailed argument was presented, but for the most part they were only refinements or elaborations of what he had already stated by the end of 1524. Moreover, although Zwingli did not engage in direct debate with Luther till 1527, he did implicitly attack Luther's views in the letter to Matthew Alber, for Alber's position represents Luther's in many ways.

Luther had already rejected what he was to see as Zwingli's position in his rejection of Hoen's letter (for example in *The Adoration of the Sacrament* in 1523) and in his attack on Carlstadt's views. Luther was indeed to see Zwingli essentially in terms of Carlstadt, and this made it difficult for him to understand Zwingli in his own terms. There were important differences between Zwingli and Carlstadt, including Zwingli's rejection of Carlstadt's view that with the word 'this' in 'This is my body' Christ pointed to his own body. However Zwingli did see Carlstadt as on his side in putting the emphasis on faith as faith in Christ (and not faith in the sacrament).

The Controversy with Luther

In the many expositions of the eucharist from *A Commentary* in 1525 to the Marburg Colloquy in 1529 Zwingli largely defended and reaffirmed what he had already said, though with some development and addition. There were two issues that underlay the discussion: whether Christ is bodily present and whether he is bodily eaten; but the concern was mostly with the latter. For Zwingli Luther put 'the chief point of salvation in the bodily eating of the body of Christ', which Luther saw as strengthening faith and remitting sins. This led Zwingli to contrast two ways of salvation: the one by eating the flesh of Christ and the other by believing in him. He opposed the first as it made the atoning death of Christ unnecessary and would also restore the papacy and a religion of externals. (Z IV 817.19–27; V 500.1–16.)

Zwingli attacked the bodily eating of the body of Christ on two grounds: faith and scripture. By faith he meant the kind of faith which leads to salvation. By scripture he meant the whole range of scriptural argument (the use of tropes, the collation of passages of scripture, the analogy and agreement between different parts of scripture, and of course the emphasis on certain key passages).

The argument from faith was in terms of faith in Christ as Son of God and not, as Luther made it, a belief about the body of Christ in the bread. Zwingli argued that salvation was promised to faith and not to bread, whereas Luther's view implied that there are two ways of salvation: the death of Christ and bodily eating. (Indeed the character of faith tells against Luther, because faith has no need of bodily food, since John's gospel says 'the one who believes in Christ will not hunger or thirst'.) For Zwingli the subject of the eucharist is the death of Christ, not the eating of the body, for the words 'Do this in remembrance of me' refer to giving thanks for Christ's death, his body given for us, and not to the eating of the body. Luther's view would make the death of Christ unnecessary, since the disciples shared in the eucharist before Christ died. (Z V 576.1–7, 659.4–661.6, 707.3–708.13, 572.27–573.2, 706.5–11.)

Faith is also the fundamental criterion in interpreting scripture. Luther had used this principle in rejecting the pope's interpretation of Matt. 16: 18 to prove that Peter was the foundation of the church. Zwingli now used this principle against Luther, arguing that the plain sense of a passage is not always the true sense. The true sense is discerned by faith and by a comparison with other relevant passages of scripture. (Z V 663.9–29, 710.2–10, 731.25–732.11.)

Besides the argument from faith, there was the argument from scripture. A vital part in this was played by St John's gospel. It was fundamental for Zwingli's understanding of the eucharist, initially in the use of John 6 and passages such as John 1: 18 and 3: 6, but later in giving examples of alloiosis, that is the sharing or interchange of properties. Zwingli spoke of John as the noblest part of the New Testament. If you take it away 'you take the sun from the world'. (Z V 564.6–16.)

John 6: 63 was his key text. He used it in support of 'is' meaning 'signifies' and so against the bodily presence of Christ as well as against bodily eating. In it Christ cut the knot 'with an axe so sharp and solid that no one can have any hope that these two pieces—body and eating—can come together again'. (In this text Zwingli's emphasis moves from 'it is the Spirit who gives life' to 'the flesh is of no avail'.) He defended his interpretation of it against Luther's view that the flesh refers not to Christ's flesh but to a fleshly understanding. He added moreover that the fathers were on his side. (Z V 616.9–15, 605.9–612.34.) As earlier he also argued that John 6: 56, which speaks of those who eat Christ's flesh as abiding in him and he in them, cannot refer to sacramental eating, as many people eat the body of Christ sacramentally and yet are not in him nor he in them. (Compare Z III 780.28–782.22.)

The discussion of alloiosis or the sharing or interchange of properties is related to the sharp distinction Zwingli makes between the divinity and humanity of Christ. (It was in 1526 that Zwingli first used the argument from the two natures of Christ.) According to his divine nature, he is omnipresent and so he is always at the right hand of the Father; whereas according to his human nature, he is not and so after his resurrection he ascended into heaven. However if his body is in heaven, it cannot be in the eucharist. For Zwingli if you make a proper distinction between the two natures, you can reconcile apparently conflicting passages, such as 'I am with you always' which refers to the divine nature, and 'you will not always have me' which refers to the human nature. (Z IV 827.4–830.28.)

He holds that Luther confuses the two natures and that that confusion underlies Luther's holding that the body of Christ is everywhere, whereas in fact Christ's body belongs to his humanity and shares the characteristics of his humanity, which can be in only one place at one time. For Zwingli a proper understanding of John's gospel requires an understanding of alloiosis, by which when speaking of one nature in Christ, we use terms that belong to the other. Thus when Christ said 'My flesh is food indeed', the word flesh applies to the human nature, but by interchange is used here of the divine, for it is as Son of God that he is food for the soul. Zwingli is concerned that the two natures should keep their distinctiveness and integrity and the appeal to alloiosis was a support in this. (Z V 683.11–701.18.)

For Zwingli it is clear from scripture that the body of Christ, including his resurrection body, was always in one place at one time and was never in more than one place at one time. Although both Zwingli and Luther engaged in philosophical argument in support of their different positions on this point, Zwingli's fundamental objection to Luther's view was biblical and theological rather than philosophical. He saw Luther as denying that Christ was human as we are, in opposition to passages such as Phil. 2: 7 and Heb. 2: 14, 17 and 4: 15, as well as denying the passages which state or imply that his body is in one place. Zwingli cited a growing range of texts about the resurrection and ascension of Christ as well as the three clauses in the creed about ascending into heaven, sitting down on the right hand of God, and coming again in glory, to show that Christ will not be here bodily until he comes again in glory to judge the living and the dead.

Both Luther and Zwingli used various analogies (sometimes the same ones) in illustration of their position. Thus Zwingli spoke of the sun which shines throughout the world, without being in each place, to show how Christ can shine everywhere by divine power while his body is in one place (Z VI ii. 167.18–168.13). The whole thrust of his argument that the body of Christ can be in only one place at one time (that means now at the right hand of God) is to demonstrate that his body cannot be in the eucharist. He described Luther's opposite view as Marcionite, in effect asserting that the body of Christ was not a real body.

Zwingli offered a host of supporting arguments in favour of his view that 'this is' means 'this signifies'. A major one is the parallel with the passover. This came to him as from God in a dream in 1525. The force of the example comes from the fact that the passover foreshadows the death of Christ and that Christ himself is the true passover. He held that the disciples who celebrated the passover each year would understand the words 'This is my body' in the light of 'The lamb is the passover'. He argued moreover by analogy with the passover that the eucharist was given for commemoration and thanksgiving and not for bodily eating. (Z IV 482.32–487.9, 844.3–847.2.)

Other arguments were drawn from the way in which the bread was still called bread and the wine was still called wine after the words of institution and from the fact that the disciples were calm rather than amazed at the Last Supper (Z IV 847.3–848.11). Zwingli also used the argument of his colleague, Heinrich Engelhard, that in the New Testament the term the body of Christ is used in three senses only: for the natural body with which Christ lived and died, for the risen body, and for the mystical body, the church. For differing reasons the bread could not be any of these. (Z IV 476.4–478.11.) The argument of his opponents that if God is omnipotent he could cause the bread to be both real bread and real flesh is dismissed by denying that something is done by God simply because he can do it. Zwingli states that God's omnipotence is always in keeping with his word. (Z IV 831.23–30. Compare Z V 501.23–6.)

The Marburg Colloquy

The differences between Luther and Zwingli on the eucharist were a serious cause of division among Protestants, a division made more serious by the stand of Roman Catholic territories after the Diet of Speyer in 1529. The cause of the Reformation was put at risk in many places and therefore the concern for Protestant unity was intensified. Philip of Hesse arranged a colloquy in the hope of attaining unity. Luther was reluctant to attend but saw it as an opportunity to convince his opponents. By contrast Zwingli was eager for the colloquy, but he also saw it as an opportunity to convince his opponents. The mediating approach of Bucer, Oecolampadius, and Melanchthon was an important factor in leading to the colloquy and to the measure of agreement at Marburg. When the participants assembled, Luther and Zwingli did not meet with each other at first, but Luther met with Oecolampadius and Zwingli with Melanchthon in the hope of creating a better atmosphere and basis for discussion.

Nothing new in Zwingli's or Luther's eucharistic theology emerged in the discussion, which was dominated, as the controversy had been till then, by Luther's insistence on the words 'This is my body'. They did not change their positions. Indeed they could not because their positions reflected their underlying theology. The colloquy produced agreement on fourteen of the fifteen articles, which were drawn up by Luther; and the disagreement in the fifteenth article on the eucharist (in only one point out of its six) was kept to a subordinate clause. (It concerned the bodily presence of Christ.) Yet the agreement at Marburg on five points in the eucharist is in a way misleading, for in three points of the five Zwingli and Luther understood the words differently or gave the emphasis to different words or phrases.

The controversy had hardened positions. From the beginning Luther had seen Zwingli in terms of Carlstadt and therefore as a spiritualist, emptying the sacraments of their power. Zwingli presented his views largely in opposition to Lutheran and Catholic views, and he increasingly tended virtually to identify the two. That made reconciliation for Zwingli other than on his terms almost impossible as any other agreement would have seemed to the Swiss a return to Catholicism. Their Catholic opponents for their part sought to intensify the division between the reformers.

The colloquy ended the bitterness of the conflict, but not the division. For Luther, though not in the same way for Zwingli and those with him, the difference that remained was fundamental. For the Lutherans it was so fundamental that they could view the Zwinglians only as friends, and not as brethren in the gospel. Yet, despite all his earlier critical assertions, that was not how Zwingli saw things at the end of the colloquy. Luther refused fellowship and communion with Zwingli, Bucer, and Oecolampadius. Only pressure from Philip of Hesse made him willing to seek an agreement at all. The division was to last for over four centuries and not till the Leuenberg Concord in 1973, almost four and a half centuries later, was an agreement found which a large number of Lutheran and Reformed Churches, though not all, could accept as a basis for fellowship in word and sacrament.

The Closing Years

The immediate effect of the colloquy, however, was a decrease in controversy and a more positive expression of Zwingli's views of the eucharist. Zwingli made it clear that the bread was not mere bread, and he began to affirm terms such as presence, true, and sacramental. His more positive view can be seen in 1530 and 1531 in works like *An Account of the Faith* written for the Diet of Augsburg, *The Letter to the Princes of Germany*, written in the same context in defence of his views after Eck's attack on them, and *An Exposition of the Faith*, written for the King of France.

At this point he was more concerned to affirm the presence of Christ than to deny it. Indeed in the appendix to *An Exposition of the Faith* he asserted, 'We believe Christ to be truly present in the Supper, indeed we do not believe that it is the Lord's Supper unless Christ is present.' In support, however, he used a text that has nothing to do explicitly with the eucharist:

'Where two or three are gathered together in my name, there am I in the midst of them.' (S IV 73.36–9.) He asserted that the true body of Christ and everything done by him is present by the contemplation of faith, before denying the bodily presence and bodily eating. He could even say that he had never denied that Christ's body is truly, sacramentally, and mysteriously present in the Supper. (Z VI ii. 806.6–17; VI iii. 263.3–265.19.) As the body is present sacramentally, it can be eaten sacramentally. He distinguished eating Christ's body spiritually, which is trusting in the mercy and goodness of God through Christ, and eating it sacramentally which is eating 'the body of Christ with the mind and spirit in conjunction with the sacrament'. But without faith we do not eat sacramentally. (S IV 53.33–55.29.)

The link made between the senses and the sacraments in 1524 was developed in the later Zwingli and was given as the reason for the eucharist, whereas earlier Zwingli had spoken of it primarily in terms of testifying to others. Zwingli held not only that the eucharist does not give faith, but also that it is of no use to us without faith, which is given by the Spirit, who can act with the sacraments or without them. This raised the question of what the benefit of the sacraments is. His answer was that whereas preaching appeals to the sense of hearing, the eucharist appeals more richly to the senses. 'Then by the symbols themselves, namely the bread and wine, Christ himself is presented as it were to the eyes, so that in this way not only the hearing, but also the sight and taste see and perceive Christ, whom the mind has present within and in whom it rejoices.' The devil tempts us through the senses, but the eucharist helps to increase our faith by engaging the senses. Zwingli always insisted, however, that faith is a gift of the Spirit, and comes from him, not from the sacrament. (Z VI iii. 259.5–265.19; S IV 46.18–21, 57.12–58.5.)

With the more positive emphasis on the eucharist went a more positive reference to the bread and wine. They are signs and a sign increases in value according to the value of what it signifies, just as the wedding ring given to the queen by her husband is of more value than the gold of which it is made. The bread therefore which had been common is now divine and sacred. (Z VI iii. 271.13–272.3; S IV 56.32–46.)

There were of course other positive elements in Zwingli's thinking which do not concern the presence of Christ and which remain from the early Zwingli. For example, in *A Proposal Concerning Images and the Mass* in May 1524, he spoke of the sacrament testifying 'to all men that we are one body and one brotherhood' and of Christ's willing 'that his own shall be one, just as he is one with the Father, and for this reason he has given us the sacrament'. 'And as he gave himself for us, we also are bound to give ourselves one for the other'. (Z III 124.27–125.15.) In Zwingli's later writings the eucharist is a thanksgiving for Christ's death for us, a confession of our faith, and a commitment to our brethren to love them as Christ loved us. It is moreover a corporate act (an emphasis that particularly distinguished Zwingli from medieval practice) for as the bread comes from many grains, so the body of the church is joined together from many members. The fact that the sacrament is an oath stresses this unity.

There are many possible influences on Zwingli's understanding of the eucharist, the most obvious being Erasmus, Augustine, and Hoen. Zwingli himself spoke of his debt to Erasmus and much in him is certainly typical of Erasmus: there were the subjective, corporate, and ethical emphases; the stress on faith and commemoration; and most notably the key role of John 6: 63. But the affinity between Zwingli and Augustine is also striking. A study of Augustine's tractates on John 6 shows how close Zwingli's thought was to Augustine, as does the frequency with which he quotes from him. There are not only the elements he has in common with Erasmus (and with Augustine as well) including his Platonism, but there is also the stress in Augustine on the sovereignty of God. (At Marburg Luther admitted that Augustine and Fulgentius were on Zwingli's side.) Hoen contributed a vital element to Zwingli's in the development of his symbolic view, though his importance for Zwingli is often exaggerated. Important, though less obvious, is the continuity between the reformers and the diverse eucharistic theologies of the Middle Ages. Most elements in the reformers' eucharistic controversy can be found in the medieval tradition, though not in the same combination nor set in the same theological context.

Fundamental in Zwingli's understanding of the eucharist is that it is a sign—and it is the nature of a sign not to be the same as what it signifies. This applies both to the sacrifice of Christ and to the body of Christ. The eucharist is a memorial of the sacrifice, not the sacrifice itself; it is a sign of the body of Christ, not the body itself. The clue that came from Hoen in 1524 that 'is' means 'signifies' fitted Zwingli's view of a sacrament and enabled him to deal with the text 'This is my body' which seemed the strongest obstacle to his position. (In a letter in April 1526 to Crautwald and Schwenckfeld he argued against the word 'represent' as—unlike 'signify'—it could imply the presence of the body (Z VIII 568.1–569.9.) For him the central text was John 6: 63, 'It is the Spirit who gives life, the flesh is of no avail.' Both halves of the verse were important, even though the emphasis most often lay on the second half. The first half fitted his emphasis on the sovereignty of God, the second half his Platonism, though that is not the only way in which it was used. Zwingli dismissed any argument from the fact that Christ used these words only once, on the grounds that heaven and earth will pass away rather than a word of God (Z VIII 210.11–12). This text was a wall of bronze which nothing could shake, let alone shatter (Z III 785.40–786.1).

There is continuity in Zwingli's view of the eucharist not only in the areas which were not a source of controversy between him and Luther (the rejection of communion in one kind and the eucharist as a sacrifice), but also in Zwingli's understanding of the presence of Christ. The symbolic view which emerged clearly at the end of 1524 is implicit in his first statements in 1523. There are from the beginning elements which imply a symbolic view of the eucharist: the sacrament as a sign; a stress on the atoning death of Christ, on its being food for the soul, on salvation as dependent on faith in Christ's body and blood as given for us, on the vital role of faith, and on the Spirit as enabling faith; and the rejection of bodily eating. The more positive notes in the later Zwingli do not indicate a real shift in his position, rather a difference of emphasis. Unlike Bucer and Oecolampadius he did not link the sacraments positively to the sovereignty of God, for example, in God's making the sacraments effective for the elect or in the Spirit's bringing Christ's death to our remembrance, although there was potential for this in his theology—and in a passage not on the eucharist he spoke of the Spirit's lifting our eyes to Christ in heaven (S VI ii. 74.28–33). His Platonist opposition between flesh and spirit was an obstacle to a more positive view of the eucharist, though he did have one surprising reference in a comment on Exod. 21: 28 to being made cruel by eating the flesh of a cruel animal, which might have helped him to overcome this opposition (Z XIII 408.1–22).

Both Zwingli and Luther saw the gospel as at stake in their controversy and that made compromise impossible. Zwingli was determined to stand by the truth: 'For we do not live to this age, nor to the princes, but to the Lord.' (Z IX 340.2–4.) At the same time his admiration for Luther was clear. He was 'one of the first champions of the gospel', a David against Goliath, a Hercules who slew the Roman boar (Z V 613.12–13, 722.3–5, 723.1–2).

Zwingli, as Bucer and Oecolampadius, appealed to the early Luther, where there is a strong emphasis on the place of faith, without realizing that his position there presupposed a belief in the real presence. The real presence was vital for Luther's understanding of God's gracious dealing with us in Jesus Christ. The sacraments offer us salvation and therefore to dispute the real presence is to dispute the way God offers us salvation. There were other differences which underlay their differences here: in christology, with Zwingli's emphasis on the distinction of the natures and Luther's on the unity of the person; in anthropology with Zwingli's frequent Platonist opposition of outward and inward in the terms flesh and Spirit, and Luther's seeing no opposition of outward and inward in them.

For Zwingli the salvation of men and women was at stake—hence the vigour of his opposition to bodily eating. If you allow that bodily eating, which is possible for believer and unbeliever alike, is a means of grace, then for Zwingli faith in God will be replaced by faith in the sacrament, and so the entire doctrine of God, Father, Son, and Holy Spirit will be overthrown. Salvation will then be put at our disposal, for we can do (or have done to us) something which mediates salvation, as it is we who administer and receive the sacrament, in which there is salvation—and that denies the sovereignty of God in our salvation. Moreover Christ's humanity and saving work are denied, for the bodily presence of Christ in the sacrament would imply that his body unlike ours can be in more places than one at a time, and bodily eating would call in question the necessity of Christ's death for salvation, as the disciples ate the Last Supper before Christ died. The role of the Spirit in our salvation is also denied, for it is the Spirit, and not the sacrament, who was given to take the place of Christ's bodily presence with mankind, and it is the Spirit, and not the sacrament, who gives faith.

11

The Church

THE changed understanding that Zwingli had of Christ and the gospel led to a changed understanding of the church. At the first disputation in January 1523 the articles on the church came immediately after those on Christ. What was said about Christ determined what was said about the church. It was described and defined in terms of him. At this stage Zwingli maintained his view against Catholic opponents, but within months he was to be challenged by some of his more radical supporters in his understanding of the church.

Christ and the Church

Already in a letter in April 1522 and in *The Petition* in July 1522 Zwingli had spoken of the church in terms of those who believe in Christ and who receive the Holy Spirit. In this he was dissenting from a view of the church as the hierarchy, as he was to do explicitly at the first disputation. In the eighth article he maintained: 'From this it follows first that all who live in the head are members and children of God and that is the church or communion of saints, the bride of Christ, the catholic church.' (Z I 459.3–5.)

This definition reflects the major points of disagreement with his Catholic opponents—by its reference to the head of the church and to the holiness and catholicity of the church.

The head of the church is Christ and Christ's headship is set in opposition to the pope as the head of the church (Z II 54.12–23). Thus the members of the church are 'all who live in the head'; it is not those who are in communion with the bishop of Rome. Parallel in some ways to the contrast between Christ and the pope is the contrast between Christ and the bishops. Far from the church's being defined in terms of the bishops, Christ is the true bishop and he is in fact freeing people from the bishops, as he has freed the people of Zurich from the Bishop of Constance. (Z V 79.3–9.)

Unlike the church defined in terms of Christ, the church defined in terms of the pope or bishops is fallible. It 'has often gone wrong and erred' (Z I 537.9; *Selected Works* 85). Bishops indeed, like anyone else, are members of the church only in so far as they have Christ as their head. The church that does not err is the one that is related to Christ and the Spirit. The Spirit moreover is not the automatic possession of the church, as many assumed. He is not present simply where a council or the representative church is assembled, but only where the word of God is master (Z II 62.21–8). Yet Zwingli could speak with confidence about the church, and in 1526 wrote that God does not abandon his church or allow it to err in the essential matters of salvation, although it may err in outward things (Z V 72.8–74.5).

The Church: One, Holy, Catholic

The traditional marks of the church (as one, holy, catholic, and apostolic) are all related to Christ. They all feature in the early Zwingli, but in the first disputation the main concern is with catholicity. Zwingli accepted two meanings of the word church in scripture: the communion of all those who believe in Christ and particular congregations or parishes. The church is both catholic or universal and local.

Zwingli discussed the catholicity of the church in expounding the articles and in *The Canon of the Mass* in 1523 and in *A Reply to Emser* in the following year. He distinguished the catholic or universal church from the Roman church for the Roman church is a local church not the universal church. The catholic church is both scattered throughout the world and gathered together in one body by the Spirit. It does not come together visibly here on earth, although it will do so at the end of the world. As Augustine and Luther, Zwingli spoke of the church as visible to Christ, but invisible to us. It is discerned only by faith. Nevertheless a person may know of himself that he is in the church, if he puts all his trust in God through Jesus Christ. (Z II 59.1–64.20, 570.19–572.31; compare Z III 252.23–269.6.)

The local church is the congregation, and together all these local churches are the catholic or universal church. It is fed by the word and nourished by the sacrament. It is the local church which removes the impenitent and receives back the penitent. Here Zwingli distinguished between those who called themselves believers and those who are believers. Although some might use the word 'church' to include the evil, Zwingli did not include them, for he regarded the evil as unbelievers rather than as believers who lapse. The local church exercises discipline and makes decisions about pastors and doctrine. An example of this is the church in Corinth, of which we read in 1 Cor. 14. (Z II 572.20–31; III 261.18–264.4.)

In the first of the two biblical uses of the term 'church' (the communion of all those who believe in Christ), the church is also holy. It does not have any inherent holiness and its members are not holy, as some thought, by virtue of being priests or religious, but it is holy in so far as it remains in Christ. In *A Reply to Emser* in 1524 he answered the charge that the church without spot or wrinkle no more exists than Plato's republic by saying that the holiness or purity is Christ's. Those who rely on him are without spot or wrinkle because he is without spot or wrinkle. (Z III 254.25–256.23.)

Alongside this view of the church as holy is Zwingli's view of it as mixed. Although Zwingli discussed the holiness of the church before his conflict with the anabaptists, they raised the issue for him more acutely. For them the church is holy and should be kept holy, with only those who believe belonging to it. Baptism, therefore, which gave entry to the church, was to be administered only to believers, and that excluded children. Moreover the eucharist should be celebrated only by those who believe and who live holy lives. Those whose lives are unholy should be excommunicated, so that the church remains holy.

In tackling the problem of the unholiness of the members of the church, Zwingli appealed to the Old and New Testaments, in which the word church is used of a community made up of believers and unbelievers alike, although the conduct of some of the latter made it clear that they were not in the church which is without spot or wrinkle. As early as a letter to Myconius on 24 July 1520 Zwingli used the parable of the wheat and tares about the church. In *A Reply to Emser* he used it again and the parables of the net and of the ten virgins, as well as the examples of Judas, Ananias and Sapphira (Acts 5) and Alexander the coppersmith (2 Tim. 4: 14). In using the parable of the wheat and tares against the anabaptists, Zwingli accepted Christ's command that the tares should be left until harvest. He did not seek to purify the church by seceding from it to form a pure church, as the anabaptists did, but by preaching the word.

In the controversy with the anabaptists the holiness of the church was related to its unity. Seeking to keep the church holy by withdrawing from those who are not holy breaks the unity of the church. Moreover those who seek to create a church of believers only, break the unity of children and adults in the church by excluding children from it. Zwingli expressed his concern for unity before the outbreak of the controversy in *A Solemn Exhortation* in May 1522. In it he spoke of God as willing all people to be descended from one father for the sake of unity, and of Christ as praying that his disciples might be one. We are to be one body whose head is Christ. (Z I 167.14–169.4.)

Zwingli developed his understanding of unity in a variety of contexts and in a variety of ways. In *A Solemn Exhortation* it was set in the context of the confederation, but for most of the decade it was set in the context of the anabaptist controversy. Zwingli expressed his concern in many ways—theological, liturgical, and practical.

An important theological and liturgical expression lay in the doctrine of the covenant. It originated outside the debate with the anabaptists, but it was used increasingly within that debate. The covenant made with the people of Israel was made with all the people, including children, and through this people the covenant was to extend to all peoples. From 1525 Zwingli affirmed that there is only one covenant and one people of God in the Old and New Testaments. From this he argued that children in the New Testament belong to the church as much as those in the Old Testament, and they should therefore be baptized. Thus infant baptism was a source of unity, whereas the anabaptist approach to the church and to baptism led to division. (Z IV 637.27–638.1, 641.1–3; VI i. 155.22–172.5; S VI i. 461.40–7; Z IV 641.19–26.) Like baptism the eucharist is linked with the unity of the church, for the church was instituted by Christ for unity—so that we might be united to him and to each other (Z III 227.11–228.6).

The unity of the church which is related to Christ is related also to the Spirit, for the Spirit does not separate or divide. On the contrary he binds together and draws into unity. Those who are endowed with the Spirit, therefore, do not despise sinners or separate from them, but rather do they call them from their evil and join them to themselves. (S VI i. 211.23–212.9.)

For Zwingli the anabaptists had a fundamental misconception of the church. The true church which is holy is known only to God, and therefore no one, including anabaptists, can know who truly believes. Moreover Christians should not separate themselves from those who are weak but bear with them as Paul teaches in Rom. 14. The Pauline concern for the weak frequently distinguishes Zwingli's more cautious approach to change from that of the anabaptists.

He saw their divisiveness not only in their particular stress on the faith and holiness of members of the church, but also in their individualism. That led him to stress the role of the whole congregation as opposed to the views of one or some members of the congregation.

How dare you introduce innovations into the church simply on your own authority and without consulting the church? I speak only of those churches in which the word of God is publicly and faithfully preached. For if every blockhead who had a novel or strange opinion were allowed to gather a sect around him, divisions and sects would become so numerous that the Christian body which we now build up with such difficulty would be broken to pieces in every individual congregation. Therefore no innovations ought to be made except with the common consent of the church and not merely of a single person. For the judgement of scripture is not mine or yours but the church's (1 Cor. 14). (Z IV 254.24–255.3; LCC xxiv. 158.)

In the middle and later 1520s, when the doctrine of election began to play a part in Zwingli's theology, it also began to feature in his description of the church. In his later writings the church was still described in terms of faith, but also in terms of election which underlies faith. References to election, however, in descriptions or definitions of the church safeguarded both the fact that the church includes children as well as adults and the fact that its origins lie in God and not in us.

An Account of the Faith begins by defining the church in terms of the elect, but goes on to speak of those who are members of the church as having faith and therefore 'they only who have firm and unwavering faith know that they are its members'. Zwingli distinguished the church which is perceived with the senses from the church of the elect which is known only to God. The members of the visible church confess Christ and participate in the sacraments, but some of them 'in heart either are averse to him or ignorant of him'. We cannot tell whether those who confess Christ are in reality believers, any more than the apostles could. Those who confess Christ are, however, baptized and become members of the church. Like Peter in his first epistle, we apply terms like elect to this church because we, unlike God, judge by the confession they make. (Z VI ii. 800.16–801.30; Jackson 464; *Works* ii. 44.)

Excommunication

The mixed character of the church raised for Zwingli—as for the church through the ages—the issue of discipline and excommunication. This became a point of dispute with the anabaptists, but it was a point of dispute before that as Zwingli criticized the practice of the medieval church.

It arose initially in the context of Luther, and Zwingli told Myconius in July 1520 that through the pontifical commissary he had tried to persuade the pope not to excommunicate Luther (Z VII 343.33–344.8). But Zwingli himself also faced the possibility of excommunication. That, almost certainly, apart from anything else would have made him consider the nature and basis of excommunication. This led him to advance two articles at the first disputation. 'That no private person may excommunicate anyone, but only the church, that is, the community of those among whom the person to be excommunicated lives, together with the watchman, that is, the minister.' 'That one may excommunicate only the person who causes public offence.' (Z I 462. 6–9.)

Here as elsewhere Zwingli sought a scriptural foundation for doctrine and practice. For him the basis of excommunication was in Christ's words in Matt. 18: 15–18. From this passage Zwingli saw the reason for excommunication as concern 'not to infect or ruin the whole body'. But excommunication is not just for keeping the church whole, it is concerned as well with the repentance of the sinner, as the example of Paul shows, where Paul exhorted the congregation to forgive the man who was penitent. He also argued that it was to be used for an offence against the church rather than one against an individual, and that the offence must be a public offence. It was not, for example, to be a way for bishops to collect debts, as happened in the medieval church. Moreover, excommunication is also not to be the prerogative of an individual, whether pope or bishop, but of the church. However as the word 'church' is used in only two senses in the New Testament, the word must mean the local church and not the universal church, for it is not possible for the universal church, to come together in one place as Matt. 18 requires. (Z II 277. 1–284. 13.)

After dealing with excommunication in the articles at the first disputation, Zwingli dealt with civil authority. In his exposition of article forty on the power of the magistrate to take life, he quoted Matt. 18 and applied it to the magistrate, although he allowed that its primary reference was to excommunication. He argued that the magistrate can take the life of those guilty of public offence, if their remaining alive would harm the body of Christ. Zwingli held that it is better for one member to perish than the whole body, and thus in taking this action the magistrate is a servant of God. (Z II 334. 24–335. 19.)

These views were advanced by Zwingli to challenge the practice of the medieval church and they show characteristic reformation and reforming insights—in the return to scripture, in the emphasis on the church rather than the hierarchy, and in the purposes for which excommunication is given (for the church's wholeness and the individual's salvation). But they show an element that was later to be characteristic of Zwingli and Zurich rather than other parts of the Reformed tradition: the role of the magistrate in discipline.

In *A Commentary* Zwingli challenged the Catholic view of excommunication by pointing out that Jesus had said, 'Tell it to the church' and not 'Tell it to the pope' (Z III 879. 35–6). (Interestingly he says in the same passage that the power of excommunication belongs not to the magistrate but to the whole church.) Later Oecolampadius was to challenge Zwingli's view, with its growing role for the magistrate, by declaring that Jesus said, 'Tell it to the church' not 'Tell it to the magistrate' (Z XI 129. 2–130. 9). Zwingli supported his view from various parts of scripture, such as the way rulers were called shepherds in Israel and the understanding of presbyter in Acts 15 as applying not only to those who preside over the word but also to councillors and senators (Z IX 455. 21–456. 8). This co-operative role for the magistrate led to changes in practice in Zurich. With *The Zurich Marriage Ordinance* in 1525 the council appointed a tribunal of six judges (two ministers and four members of the council) to deal with matrimonial and other matters. In the case of adultery the ministers were to excommunicate and the magistrates were to deal with corporal punishment and property. However in 1526 it was the council alone which dealt with adultery.

In his last major work, *An Exposition of the Faith*, Zwingli saw the role of the magistrate in discipline as vital to the life of the church, relating it to his being one of the shepherds of the church. Indeed half the brief article on the church is devoted to the place of the magistrate in the discipline of the church.

Consequently the visible church contains within itself many who are insolent and hostile, thinking nothing of it if they are excommunicated a hundred times, seeing they have no faith. Hence there arises the need of government for the punishment of flagrant sinners.... Seeing, then, that there are shepherds in the church, and amongst them we may number princes, as may be seen from Jeremiah, it is evident that without government a church is maimed and impotent. ... we teach that government is necessary to the completeness of the body of the church. (S IV 58.42–59.4; LCC xxiv. 266; *Works* ii. 261.)

In his understanding of the role of the magistrate in the church Zwingli differed not only from reformers such as Oecolampadius but also from the anabaptists. They were seeking in their different ways forms of independence for the church. The anabaptists believed in the total separation of the church from the civil power, with the magistrate being concerned with those outside the church and having no part in the church's reform or discipline. Excommunication was the means whereby the church was kept pure and it was essential for that purpose. The second article of *The Schleitheim Confession* in 1527 stated: 'The ban shall be employed with all those who have given themselves to the Lord, to walk in his commandments, and with all those who are baptized into the one body of Christ and who are called brethren and sisters, and yet who slip sometimes and fall into error and sin, being inadvertently overtaken.' It is to take place 'before the breaking of bread, so that we may break and eat one bread, with one mind and in one love, and may drink of one cup'. The fourth article affirmed the separation of believer and unbeliever, good and evil, while the sixth asserted that the sword is ordained of God 'outside the perfection of Christ'. 'In the perfection of Christ, however, only the ban is used for a warning and for the excommunication of the one who has sinned, without putting the flesh to death.'[1]

In associating excommunication with the eucharist the anabaptists were like Zwingli. In *Excommunication from the Eucharist* in 1525 he made proposals to introduce it in that context, in connection with the re-ordering of the service. A number of public sins, such as adultery, prostitution, drunkenness, and blasphemy, as well as graver sins, were considered grounds for what amounted to the greater excommunication, exclusion from social intercourse as well as from communion. (Z IV 186. 26–187. 2.)

[1] H. J. Hillerbrand, *The Protestant Reformation* (London, 1968) 131–4.

As Zwingli developed his doctrine of election, new questions arose about the practice of excommunication, as it could mean that the church was excommunicating those whom God had elected, which would contradict the words of Christ that what was bound on earth would be bound in heaven. Zwingli tackled this in his commentaries and in connection with the Berne disputation. He held that the church was following what God had already done. For him those whom the church excommunicated have already been rejected by God, and when the church receives back the penitent, then the church is again following God's action, for the penitence is a sign of divine grace (Z VI i. 258. 9–260. 14). Our action in excommunication does not affect a person's election, which is entirely in God's hands. However if a person is elect, he will repent.

The Ministry

Zwingli's understanding of the ministry as his understanding of the church was affected by his understanding of Christ and the gospel. In articles sixty-one and sixty-two, as Luther before him, he rejected the medieval notion of the indelible character of ordination as not scriptural and not present in the early church before Jerome. For him, as for Luther, someone could be dismissed who was not suited to the office of a minister, just as for example a mayor could be who did not look after peace and justice. (Z II 438. 14–440. 16.) He also repudiated the sacrificial view of the ministry, as a denial of Christ's once for all sacrifice for sin and of Christ's being a priest for ever. By contrast, like Luther, he asserted the priesthood of all believers.

He attacked both the exercise of temporal power by the ministers of the church and the misuse of the ministerial office for financial gain, for example in the abuse of excommunication and the sale of masses. By contrast with the medieval view of the priest, he asserted that a priest is to be 'an honourable proclaimer of the word of God and a guardian for the salvation of souls' (Z II 439. 17–18; *Writings* i. 355). Proclaiming the word includes the care and visiting of the poor, the sick, and the needy as 'all these things belong to the word of God' (Z II 441. 7–12).

Preaching is at the heart of the ministry, and the word of God which is preached was for Zwingli as for Luther both law and gospel, 'for in it we learn what God demands of us and with what grace he comes to our aid' (Z II 494. 10–13). The central role of preaching can be seen in Zwingli's own ministry in Zurich, where the great emphasis was on preaching. It can be seen also in his concern for others to be ministers of the word. At the second disputation at which several hundred ministers were present, he preached on the ministry. The sermon was later published as *The Shepherd* (Z III 5–68). It portrayed the true shepherd over against the false shepherd, as one whose life reflects God's glory and the needs of the sheep, and whose word is God's not his own. But perhaps most striking is the prophetic character of the shepherd as he challenges both high and low alike, not only in religious matters but also in matters as diverse as greed, usury, war, the mercenary system, and monopolies. The wide range of concern is typical of Zwingli's own preaching that touched every aspect of the life of the people.

With the growth of the radicals after the second disputation and especially after the rebaptisms in 1525, Zwingli's attack shifted to them. He dealt with them and their practice of the ministry in June 1525 in *The Ministry*. If his Catholic opponents erred in separating priest and people and in ascribing to the priest a character and role he did not have, his radical opponents erred in not recognizing the place of the ordained ministry and in not seeing that there is a distinction between church members and ministers. He argued that Christ appointed some to the ministry but not all, for as the New Testament bears witness not all were apostles, prophets, or teachers (Z IV 419.7–420.2). Zwingli attacked anabaptists for entering parishes without permission and—from his point of view—for creating confusion and disturbance by what they did and taught (Z IV 383.4–8).

Fundamental in Zwingli's detailed attack on them from the New Testament was the view that a person may not presume to take the ministerial office upon himself, but must be commissioned by God and the church (Z IV 421.19–22). Zwingli also attacked their ignorance of the Bible and their false claims to the Spirit. He used the example of someone who insisted on entering the pulpit and preaching, but who did not understand part of the biblical passage and who in the end was made by the congregation to give way. Yet such people claimed to have the Spirit. (Z IV 420.3–24.)

Zwingli's understanding of prophecy in terms of the biblical languages made him challenge the anabaptists' lack of learning and hence their incapacity for the ministry. Hubmaier in reply accused Zwingli of creating a new popery, for dependence on those versed in the biblical languages was like the earlier dependence on popes and councils (Z IV 601.1–602.4 and 601 n. 8). Simon Stumpf, another of the radicals, rejected paid full-time ministers in favour of those who possessed the German bible and the Holy Spirit (Z VI i. 559 n. 15). Zwingli however held that if knowledge of the biblical languages were to be lost again, then the church would be back in its former darkness. He also argued in favour of a paid ministry, as the alternative to it would be begging, with the risk of greed in the case of some preachers and of flattery rather than prophetic preaching in the case of others. (Z IV 403.30–405.19, 415.2–17.)

The development of the prophecy in June 1525 shaped a distinctively Reformed model of ministry in opposition to that of both Catholic and anabaptist. It stressed the preaching of the word (in contrast to the priestly view of his Catholic opponents) and the scriptures as the criterion of the Spirit (in contrast to the anabaptist claim to have the Spirit). The word 'prophet' became the dominant term for the minister in the mid-1520s although other terms are used which have a slightly different emphasis, such as bishop and pastor. The word 'prophet' is an inclusive term as the word of God, of which the prophet is a minister, includes word and sacraments, presiding and pastoral care. The ministry is so central to the life of the church that Zwingli could say in *An Account of the Faith*:

> The work of prophecy or preaching I believe to be most holy, so that above any other duty it is in the highest degree necessary. For in speaking canonically or regularly we see that among all nations the outward preaching of apostles and evangelists or bishops has preceded faith. (Z VI ii. 813.7–13; Jackson 478; *Works* ii. 56.)

12

The State

THE relation of church and state in Zwingli is represented and misrepresented in the statue by the Wasserkirche in Zurich, where he stands with the Bible in one hand and the sword in the other.

It represents the relationship in expressing the fact that church and state are not two separate communities, but one and the same community under the sovereign rule of God. That meant that the minister and the magistrate are concerned with the whole life of the community and not just part of it. In this each is the servant of God.

It misrepresents the relationship by implying that the minister can also be the magistrate. However the role of each is different. The Bible or the word of God was God's instrument in the hands of the minister, as the sword is God's instrument in the hands of the magistrate. For Zwingli they belong together, but not in the same person.

Zwingli did not think that it was the role of the minister to wield the sword, although he himself died on the field of battle wielding one. He thought that it was exceptional for someone to be like Samuel in the Old Testament both a prophet and a ruler. But he did think that the sword was a proper instrument not only to protect the good but also to protect the gospel. His death was in a battle whose aim was to protect the preaching of the gospel. He was present as chaplain but nevertheless he did not hesitate to fight with his soldiers when he saw them outnumbered. This aim and this action distinguished him sharply not only from Luther, who regarded Zwingli's death on the field of battle as God's judgement on him, but also from Calvin and other reformers.

The statue leads into the controversial question of the relation of church and state in Zwingli, with its differences from Luther and also from later Reformed thinking. First, however, we may note Zwingli's own development especially up to the disputation in January 1523, as this shaped his understanding of church and society.

Zwingli's Development

Zwingli's differences from Luther both in approach and practice as a reformer need to be placed in the context of his own development before he went to Zurich at the end of 1518 and in the setting of his ministry in Zurich. As a boy, before he was subject to the influence of Swiss humanism, with its strong sense of patriotism, and before he had read Erasmus and Marsilius of Padua who influenced his views, Zwingli claimed that he was strongly patriotic (Z V 250.8–11). There is certainly clear evidence of his patriotism as a young man. His earliest writings, before he became a reformer, reveal a person with a passionate love of his native land and a longing for liberty. These led to his fierce opposition to the mercenary service which entangled the Swiss in the service of foreign powers. This was expressed in allegorical form in *The Ox*, a poem written as early as 1510.

This opposition to mercenary service was probably increased by his own experience of war. He may have gone with the troops as a chaplain in 1512, and if he did, the account he gave of engagements between the Swiss and the French was a firsthand account and not just a report of what others had said. He certainly went in 1513 and 1515, and in September 1515 he witnessed the disastrous battle at Marignano, in which thousands of Swiss soldiers died. These experiences intensified his sense of the devastation of war, and the moral and social cost to his own people. He wrote another allegorical poem *The Labyrinth* in 1516, in a further attack on the mercenary system. This time under the influence of Erasmian humanism there was an explicitly religious dimension to his patriotism.

Thus from the start, before he became fully a reformer, Zwingli's ministry and theology were set in a framework that was social and political, indeed national and international, and not simply individual and religious. It was, moreover, his opposition to mercenary service, and in particular the French alliance, that caused him to leave Glarus for Einsiedeln in 1516. It was also a factor later in his invitation to Zurich, for there was opposition to mercenary service and the French alliance in Zurich long before his arrival there.

With his deeper grasp of the Christian faith, in the beginning of the 1520s, Zwingli saw war and mercenary service in theological and not just moral terms. Mercenary warfare had many dangers. It led to the perverting of justice through bribes; it encouraged envy and luxury; it tended to the exercise of power by foreign rulers. But the greatest danger was that it brought God's wrath on the people. (Z I 175–85). For Zwingli therefore the gospel was related to God's wrath in a national and not just, as for Luther, in an individual sense.

As a reformer he saw that it was the gospel that brought in its train the abolition of mercenary service. This did not mean that the gospel served political ends, but that it had political effects. In 1522 he wrote, 'For Zurich more than any other of the Swiss cantons is in peace and quiet, and this all good citizens put down to the credit of the gospel.' (Z I 148. 32–3; *Selected Works* 16; *Works* i. 121.) 'I do not deny, nay, I assert, that the teachings of Christ contribute very greatly to the peace of the state, if indeed they are set forth in their purity.' (Z I 308. 24–6; *Works* i. 267.)

This is the understanding of the Christian ministry and the Christian message which developed in Zwingli both before he came to Zurich at the end of 1518 and in his first years there. His development was different from that of Luther. Luther's life as a monk and his sense of God's judgement on his personal life were quite different from Zwingli's life as a parish priest and army chaplain and his sense of God's judgement on his people.

There was a difference not only in their ministry and in their experience, but also in the political and geographical circumstances in which their ministries were exercised. Luther worked in Saxony with a single ruler, Frederick the Wise, who was one of the electors in the Holy Roman Empire. Zwingli worked in a city-state within the Swiss confederation with rule exercised by a council. The pattern of government in Zurich and the size of the city made it possible and on occasion necessary for Zwingli to involve himself actively in the affairs of the city. This both expressed and helped to account for some of his differences from Luther.

His understanding therefore of the relations of church and state or of minister and magistrate was not simply theoretical. His practice moreover was likely to have affected his theory as theory did his practice. As with all men of affairs his teaching and practice did not always coincide. His teaching was rooted in the Bible, but it was also influenced by his reading of Christian and non-Christian writers, particularly Aristotle. We may properly distinguish what he said from what he did, and recognize that what he did was inevitably conditioned in part by the circumstances he faced, in particular the situation in Zurich and the confederation.

The Role of the Council

The city council had an important role in the Reformation in Zurich, as can be seen in what it did but also in the way Zwingli understood it. From the beginning of his ministry in Zurich he saw that the council had a vital part in the reformation of the church. In part this was a recognition of the increasingly independent role it had already played in church affairs, though not in matters of doctrine and worship; but in part it was the recognition with so many others that if the bishops would not reform the church then the civil power (whether emperor, prince, or council) would have to do so. From the beginning therefore the council had an indispensable role in the Reformation in Zurich.

It was the council which summoned the first disputation in January 1523 and which at the end both judged that Zwingli's preaching was in accordance with scripture and required that all other preaching be scriptural. However Zwingli saw the assembly, which the council had summoned at his instigation 'in order to stop great unrest and disunity', as 'a Christian assembly', not as a civil gathering. (Z I 484.11–14, 495.7–11.) (This suggests comparison with councils in the early church.) The council also summoned the second disputation. At the end it accepted the case made by the reformers that the mass and images were unscriptural. Then with the approval of Zwingli and others, though not that of the radicals, it was left to the council to determine when the mass and images were to be abolished.

The growing role of the council was related to political circumstances in Zurich and the confederation. The disturbances caused by the anabaptists in Zurich and beyond, the opposition of Catholics in Zurich but even more in the other cantons, the alliances forged by his Catholic opponents, such as the league formed by Lucerne, Zug, Uri, Schwyz, and Unterwalden at Beckenried in April 1524, all these led to a growing involvement of Zwingli in the affairs of the city and the growing role for the council in the affairs of the church. Among other things the council played a part in excommunication, in requiring baptism (1525) and church attendance (1529), and in instituting ordinances about marriage and social behaviour.

It is, however, important to see how Zwingli understood the role of the council and not simply what it did in practice. In any case its role was not determined by political necessity, although it was undoubtedly influenced by it. Zwingli's understanding of its role was rooted in the Bible and the history of the church. It was part of his unified vision of society as under the sovereign rule of God, within which minister and magistrate have distinct but not separate roles. Each aids the other in his God-given role. The minister (or prophet as Zwingli increasingly described him) helps the magistrate by the preaching of the word, and the magistrate (the council in the case of Zurich) helps the minister.

In the first disputation in 1523 Zwingli saw one of the main tasks of the council as permitting the preaching of the gospel. That was not an act external to the church, but one which showed that the council if properly authorized could act within the church. In expounding the thirty-sixth article Zwingli discussed 1 Cor. 6, a passage used by Catholics to support papal courts. Zwingli argued that it was concerned with bringing disputes before Christians rather than before judges who were non-Christian. As the princes under whom Christians live are Christian, it is from them that Christians should seek judgement. (This is an early example, Heb. 13: 17 being another, where Zwingli ascribed to temporal rulers prerogatives which belonged in some sense to the church and its leaders or members.) The council could also act in removing members from the church for the good of the church. (Z II 310. 13–28, 313. 9–25, 324. 11–18.) In a letter to Strasbourg in December 1524 he implied that the council should take the initiative in removing preachers who do not preach the gospel or whose lives deny what they preach, and that if it did not do so the church would have to act (Z VIII 265. 25–266. 11). The developing role of the council can be seen as a natural growth from Zwingli's position in 1523 and compatible with it.

At the second disputation in October 1523 the division between Zwingli and his radical supporters became open. He would have agreed with Schmid's words that it was the council's task to help Christ back into his kingdom (Z II 797. 31–798. 8). After the mass and images had been declared unscriptural, he was like Schmid prepared to leave the pace of change to the council in order to avoid disturbance. Simon Stumpf saw this as a sign that Zwingli was leaving judgement to the council. He, however, made it clear that no one, including the council, was to make judgement on the word of God. (Z II 784. 10–26.) The expounder of that word was the minister. Zwingli manifested this in preaching on the third day of the disputation a sermon entitled *The Shepherd*, which dealt with the prophetic role of the minister.

The criteria for action by the council were: submission to the word of God, the assent of the church, the need for peace, and the furtherance of the gospel. In a digression in *The Eucharist* he responded to a charge that the reformers 'allow matters which ought to belong to the whole church to be dealt with by the Two Hundred when the church of the whole city and neighbourhood is 7,000, more or less'. Zwingli made clear his condition that the decisions have to be made under the leading of the word and that the council 'is not in place of the church except in so far as the church itself has by silent consent till now kindly accepted its deliberations and decisions'. He used the example of the church sending Paul and Barnabas to Jerusalem as a precedent for the delegation of authority in order to avoid contention. He argued that the council acted 'in the name of the church and not its own name' because it left the churches in the towns and country free in matters such as images and the celebration of the eucharist, as there was no great reason to fear contention there, the churches there not being large. Zwingli, moreover, always instructed the people beforehand in the matters to be considered by the council so that what was determined by it and the ministers had already been determined in the minds of the faithful. (Z IV 478. 10–480. 29; *Writings* ii. 206–7.)

In an important letter to Ambrosius Blarer on 4 May 1528, Zwingli stated—in contrast to Luther—that the kingdom of God is outward. He then discussed the role of the magistrate in outward things, the only area which is their sphere. His arguments included the appeal to the term elders in Acts 15: 6 as meaning councillors and senators and not only those who preside over the word. (Z IX 452. 23–458. 3.) This offered a further support for the role allowed to the council.

The need that the church has for the magistrate was made explicit in the analogy of body and soul in *An Exposition of the Faith*, 'For just as man is necessarily constituted of both soul and body, the body being the lesser and humbler part, so there can be no church without government, although government supervises and controls those more mundane circumstances which are far removed from the things of the Spirit.' (S IV 60. 4–9; LCC xxiv. 267–8; *Works* ii. 263.) In the light of Old Testament references Zwingli spoke of rulers as shepherds in the church, without whom the church would be maimed and impotent (S IV 58. 46–59. 2). The church needed government in dealing with persistent offenders. 'Consequently the visible church contains within itself many who are insolent and hostile, thinking nothing of it if they are excommunicated a hundred times, seeing they have no faith. Hence there arises the need of government for the punishment of flagrant sinners.' (S IV 58.42–6; LCC xxiv. 266; *Works* ii. 261.) There is a precedent for this in what Zwingli stated in *An Exposition of the Articles* in 1523, but it is also clearly a development, typical—as most of the developments—of a later stage in the reformation of a city and a church.

As the council had a role in relation to the church so the minister had a role in relation to the government, and in Zurich that meant to the council. At the first disputation Zwingli envisaged two major tasks of the council. The first, which bore on its relations to the life of the church, was to permit the preaching of the gospel. The second was to order the life of Zurich in accordance with God's laws. The council was no more autonomous in the second of these tasks than in the first. It was set under the sovereign rule of God and if it departed from this it was to be deposed. The forty-second and forty-third articles stated about those in government: 'Should they become unfaithful and not act according to the precepts of Christ, they may be deposed in the name of God.' 'In short, the dominion of the one who rules with God alone is the best and most stable; but the dominion of the one who rules by his own whim, is the worst and most insecure.' (Z II 342.26–8, 346.15–18; *Writings* i. 278, 281.)

For the fulfilment of its second task of ordering the life of the community in accordance with God's laws the city needed Christian councillors who accepted God's law and Christian preachers who expounded it. Zwingli argued the need for Christian leaders initially against Catholic opponents who subordinated the civil power to the bishops and the pope, but later against anabaptists who were opposed to Christians taking part in government. He argued on the basis of texts like Rom. 13: 1 that everyone (including bishops) was subject to the civil authorities, and then on the basis of Old Testament rulers and New Testament examples such as Erastus and Sergius Paulus that Christians should be in government, indeed that those most fitted to govern were Christians. Christians were fitted because they accepted God's law and would be able to interpret laws in a Christian way.

The vital role of the minister (or prophet) in society lay in preaching God's word. Zwingli spoke of the prophet as more necessary and fundamental than the magistrate. If the prophet falls short, the magistrate and people suffer; and yet one prophet who is true can rescue them. Indeed a true prophet could set up a magistrate, if there were no magistrate, though a magistrate could effect nothing, if there were not a true prophet. (S VI i. 367.15–27; Z XIV 421.4–10; S VI i. 550.21–5.) 'O happy rulers, cities, and peoples, among whom the Lord speaks freely through his servants the prophets. For thus religion can increase, innocence return, justice reign, without which what we think kingdoms and governments are robbery and violence'. (Z XIV 14.21–4.)

Zwingli stated that if the council were to prescribe any law not drawn from the scriptures, he would preach against it with God's word (Z II 775.12–16). He resisted any attempt to claim autonomy for the economic or the political sphere. In *Those Who Give Cause for Tumult*, when discussing interest and finance, he answered the question about what they had to do with the gospel simply with the words 'much in every way'. To the later question what do financial transactions, adultery, or drunkenness have to do with the minister, he replied that such a question is the same as the response of the devils when they said, 'Jesus what have we to do with you?' (Z III 423.1, 26–30.) The Old Testament model of the prophet coloured Zwingli's presentation of the ministry as prophetic, but it drew also on the ministry of Christ and the apostles in the New Testament. The prophet, like Christ, must be willing to lay down his life for the sake of the sheep. He will speak against prince, emperor, or pope not only for some obviously spiritual reason like resisting God's word, but also if they place unjust temporal burdens on the people. (Z III 26.25–27.1.) Following the example of Elijah with Ahab and Jezebel, the preacher must speak against the greatest tyrant, even where the matter concerns not the whole people but only a single individual (Z III 34.3–5). To refuse to attack greed, usury, war, the mercenary system, monopolies, and companies which harm the common good, is preaching the gospel of Christ crucified—but without the cross.

Indeed it is to be the enemy of the cross of Christ. (Z VI ii. 299.21–300.5.) For Zwingli there is a simple test of the true and false prophet. 'If a prophet looks to the glory of God, if he looks to justice, peace and the public good (*salutem*), it is certain he is a true prophet, one sent by God. If he looks to anything else, he is false.' (S VI i. 247.17–20.)

Zwingli's personal application of the role of the prophet developed beyond his theory. He was not only a preacher but also a participant in the affairs of the city in his concern for the defence of the Reformation by the council. In this there were the alliance with Basle, Berne, Strasbourg, and others in the Christian Civic Union, the negotiations with Philip of Hesse, the attempt at alliances with France and Venice, neither of them Protestant, and of course the exhortation to engage in battle with the Catholic cantons rather than use sanctions. (With his death the situation changed. The council rejected the idea that his successor would participate in civic affairs as Zwingli had done, though Bullinger insisted on the prophetic role of preaching the word in all matters that had to do with God's rule in society.)

The Role of Government

Zwingli was concerned not only with the role of the council in Zurich but also with the role of government in human society. In *An Exposition of the Articles* and *Divine and Human Righteousness* published in July 1523, Zwingli offered two presentations of the purpose of government and the obligations of government and citizens. The first developed the sixty-seven articles which Zwingli had advanced at the first disputation, in the middle of which were ten articles on government. They were therefore presented by Zwingli as part of the Christian faith which he had been preaching in Zurich. There is a contrast here with Luther's ninety-five theses which dealt solely with the narrower religious issue of indulgences. The second work, *Divine and Human Righteousness*, developed what had been preached as a sermon on 24 June, two days after a delegation from several parishes met the council to discuss various disputed matters, including the payment of tithes.

In both of these works government was set in the context of God's ordering of the world. Christians co-operate in this by their participation and obedience (or in some circumstances disobedience). These works were written at a time of considerable tension. Outside Zurich Zwingli was threatened by the federal diet with imprisonment if he entered any of the other cantons, while inside Zurich a controversy over tithes was raging. The work of the Reformation in the other cantons as well as in Zurich itself would have been imperilled by an outbreak of religious or social disorder, such as seemed possible. In this context Zwingli presented his own positive view of government, so that the preaching of the gospel could be safeguarded. He affirmed that 'the gospel of Christ is not opposed to government ... but is a support of government', but added the qualification 'as far it acts in a Christian way in accordance with the standard prescribed by God' (Z II 473.1–5).

His view of government was presented in the exposition of articles thirty-four to forty-three and with certain modifications remained constant. Like Luther he held that there would be no need of government if everyone were Christian. 'If all men gave God what they owe him, we should need no prince or ruler, indeed we should never have left paradise.' (Z II 305.26–8.) Zwingli argued about the origin of government and its purpose on the basis of texts such as Rom. 13 and a range of other passages in the Old Testament and the New.

Government has a positive and a negative purpose: to protect the good and to punish the evil. In keeping with these purposes laws must be made in conformity with God's word so that, as article thirty-nine puts it, 'they may protect the oppressed, even if he does not complain'.

Rom. 13: 1 and other passages were also used to support obedience by every soul (including the pope) to the authorities, whether they were good or evil. In this Zwingli argued initially against Catholic opponents, but then against radical opponents, in relation, for example, to paying the tithe. The obligation to obey gives way, however, to the obligation to disobey when the authorities set themselves against God, whether in commanding what is contrary to his will or in seeking to control the preaching of the word. In this context Zwingli appealed constantly to the word: 'We must obey God rather than men.' Moreover disobedience could lead to resistance and even the overthrow of a ruler if he became a tyrant. The forty-second article stated, 'If, however, they are unfaithful and deal contrary to the rule of Christ, they may be deposed with God.' Zwingli interpreted this article in terms of rulers who supported sinners rather than punished them, who oppressed the innocent, and who opposed the preaching of the gospel. (Z II 343.13–16.)

In his early insistence that tyrants should be removed Zwingli's views were markedly different from Luther's, and they were to be influential in the way Reformed theology developed. The removal was, however, to follow a proper procedure. It was not to be by murder or war or uprising, but by those who elected the ruler. That created a problem with rulers who were not elected, but Zwingli argued that with all rulers there must at some point have been the consent of the people. (Z II 342.26–8, 344.17–346.13.) Zwingli followed examples from the Old Testament in stating that God may punish us with unjust rulers, but he also used the example of Moses to show that in his mercy he wishes to liberate us as he liberated Israel. This example was used initially of liberation from the pope, but later of liberation from temporal rulers as well. (Z II 311.27–312.7; III 468.12–23, 873.32–7, 880.16–19; XIII 327.18–20.)

The sermon on *Divine and Human Righteousness* was a response to an attack by radicals on the paying of tithes and interest. They based their case on the Sermon on the Mount. Zwingli in his response made a distinction between two kinds of righteousness, divine and human. Divine righteousness which is inward is perfect conformity with the will of God. If people lived in conformity with God's will there would be no need of human righteousness (or government) which is outward. However since we do not love our neighbour, God gives other commands, concerned with our outward actions, such as not stealing. If we obeyed them, we should be righteous before men, but not necessarily before God, who knows what is in our heart.

Government cannot know that and therefore is concerned, as Paul makes clear in Rom. 13, with the outward and not the inward, with our deeds and not our thoughts. (Z II 484.21–485.14, 486.18–487.8, 503.27–33.)

Whereas the radicals argued for the abolition of tithes and private property as contrary to scripture, Zwingli defended them in terms of human righteousness. Zwingli seems radical in seeing divine righteousness as the standard by which everything is judged, social as well as personal. It is significant also that those he regarded as the true disturbers of the peace were the bishops and clergy, and also the princes, the powerful, and the wealthy in society, and not those who rebel against injustice and oppression. However, in his practical policy it was human rather than divine righteousness that prevailed, and that meant that Zwingli was in practice more conservative than his radical opponents.

There are developments in Zwingli and shifts of emphasis, but there is continuity between the early and the late Zwingli. Some of the developments obviously relate to the changing circumstances in Zurich and outside: the continued strength of the conservatives, the disturbance created by the radicals, the need to defend the Reformation, and the opportunities for the gospel to be preached in other places. However Zwingli's response both in his writings and in his actions is consistent with his earlier position, and in particular with what he said and did up to 1525, the year in which many see a change.

Some assert a shift from the New Testament to the Old. However Zwingli still preached regularly from both and if there was a growing emphasis on the Old Testament, it may relate to Zwingli's recognition that the situation in Zurich (and in general in Europe) corresponded more closely with Israel at the time of the prophets than with the church at the time of the apostles.[1] Yoder argues that after 1523 the council acted without the assent of the church in an assembly and without delegation by the church. There was, however, no formal delegation at the first disputation, and Zwingli still argued that there was silent assent

[1] J. Kessler, *Sabbata*, ed. E. Egli and R. Schoch (St Gallen, 1902), 355.18–21.

in 1525 in *The Eucharist*. A different charge made is that of legalism in applying the Bible. This must also be questioned, as—to take one example—Zwingli clearly allowed that circumstances could determine whether the biblical punishment for an offence should be increased or decreased (Z II 488.19–489.5.)

Church and society overlapped for Zwingli so closely that in answer to the question how the state differs from the church, he said that there is a difference only inwardly for 'the state can be content if you show yourself a faithful citizen, even if you do not trust in Christ'. The life of the state does not differ at all from the life of the church, for each demands what the other demands. Indeed Zwingli could refer to the Christian church as the Christian city or state. (Z III 867.13–17, 868.15–22; *Works* iii. 294.) This relationship is reflected in the respective roles of the preacher and the magistrate. The preacher is concerned with divine righteousness, which is inward and means perfect conformity with the will of God. The magistrate is concerned with human righteousness, which is outward and means words and deeds which help or at least do not harm our neighbour. Thus human righteousness is related to divine righteousness. They both help each other—the preacher by preaching the word of God, and the magistrate by protecting that preaching and by ordering the life of society in conformity with God's law. For his God-given task the magistrate has the sword, whereas the preacher has the word.

Zwingli's understanding of the state was theocratic, in the sense that the whole life of the community is under the rule of God and that the minister and magistrate are to seek to establish that rule. (For Zwingli theocracy did not mean that the state or magistrate was subject to the church or minister or that the church or minister was subject to the state or magistrate.) For him matters of social justice were not therefore at the circumference of Christian preaching but at the centre. Indeed he accused some people of preaching the gospel of Christ crucified but without the cross. They speak sweetly and cleverly of God's work, but because they are enemies of the cross of Christ, they do not attack greed, the wanton exercise of power by those in authority, the giving of false weight or false judgement, and monopolies (Z VI ii. 299.21–300.5).

His concern that the life of society and not just the life of the individual should be to the glory of God comes out in the closing words of *A Commentary*. 'All that I have said, I have said to the glory of God, and for the benefit of the commonwealth of Christ and the good of the conscience.' (Z III 911.31–1; *Works* iii. 343.) His priorities were: God, society, and the individual.

13

Zwingli: Theologian and Reformer

ZWINGLI'S theology has many characteristic marks, of which the two most notable are that it is biblical and centred in God. They are not separate, but are intimately related, for the Bible is God's word and not man's and it points to faith in God and not in man.

A Biblical Theologian

The statue of Zwingli by the Wasserkirche in Zurich portrays him with the sword held by the left hand but with the Bible held above it in the right hand. The statue rightly emphasizes the central role of the Bible in Zwingli's reforming ministry. He began his ministry in Zurich on Saturday 1 January 1519, his 35th birthday. He announced that he would begin the next day a continuous exposition of St Matthew, not according to the fathers but according to the scriptures themselves. This action of Zwingli focuses attention on the dominant element in his ministry: the exposition and proclamation of the word.

The preaching of the word meant that the Bible was not God's word in a merely static sense, as something given by God in the past. It was rather for Zwingli the living word of God. Zwingli was to write in *A Commentary*, 'Those who are faithful therefore grasp at the word of God, as a shipwrecked man grasps at a plank.' (Z III 670.33–4; *Works* iii. 93.) It was through the preaching of the word that God changed lives and changed society, for in preaching it is God who is the chief actor and not the preacher. Zwingli could therefore say of his preaching in Zurich: 'This is the seed I have sown, Matthew, Luke, Paul, and Peter have watered it, and God has given it splendid increase'. (Z I 285.25–8; *Works* i. 239.)

To the preaching was added the prophecy in June 1525. It combined scholarly exegesis with biblical exposition. It led to a flow of commentaries on the books of the Bible, and it helped to make both ministers and theological students men of the Bible. In this way Zwingli's biblical emphasis was to shape the life of the church in Zurich and beyond. It is this which was fundamental, though the prophecy is interesting for its surprisingly modern combination of ministerial and lay education and its use of a participatory style of learning. Through exegesis and exposition the Bible spoke to the life of people and their community. The prayer used at the beginning asked not only for an illumination of one's mind but also for a consequent transformation of one's life. Scholarship was not to be divorced from piety, both personal and social.

Two years earlier in the first disputation the fundamental role of the Bible in the Reformation was vividly demonstrated in another way. The Bible was placed before the assembly in Hebrew, Latin, and Greek, as a witness to the fact that the criterion of all preaching and teaching is scripture. 'I say that we have here infallible and unprejudiced judges, that is the holy writ, which can neither lie nor deceive. These we have present in Hebrew, Greek, and Latin tongues; these let us take on both sides as fair and just judges.' (Z II 498.2–6; *Selected Works* 56–7.) Moreover the sixty-seven articles which were the subject of debate at the disputation were described as being 'on the basis of scripture, which is called *theopneustos*, that is inspired by God'(Z I 458.3–6).

It was the central role and sole authority of scripture which divided Zwingli from his Catholic opponents in Zurich and beyond. With it he repudiated the authority of the church, expressed in the teaching office of the pope or bishops and in the appeal to the councils and fathers of the church. 'They are impious who embrace the word of man as God's. It is, therefore, madness and utter impiety to put the enactments and decrees of certain men or certain councils upon an equality with the word of God.' (Z III 674.23–5; *Works* iii. 98.) Nevertheless Zwingli could claim in *An Exposition of the Faith* that his teaching had the support of the fathers: 'Nor do we make a single assertion for which we have not the authority of the first doctors of the church.' (S IV 69.4–5; LCC xxiv. 278.)

Zwingli's view of scripture, above all his giving attention to the whole of it and not just to certain parts, supplied strength and comprehensiveness to his grasp of the Christian faith. It saved him from the onesidedness of the anabaptists in neglecting the Old Testament in favour of the New and of Luther in stressing justification to the detriment of sanctification.

Yet alongside the centrality of the Bible there was an astonishing, some would say an excessive, openness to the truth whether or not it came in an explicitly Christian form. Standing in a tradition that runs through Justin Martyr and Augustine, Zwingli did not hesitate to welcome the truth he saw in non-Christian writers—in his case essentially pre-Christian ones. Here one sees in him the profound and continuing influence of humanist scholarship, with its delight in the rediscovered literature of Greece and Rome. (At points, especially in his writing on providence, the priority given to the non-biblical material has raised suspicion about the genuinely biblical nature of Zwingli's theology.) Zwingli, following Augustine, held that all truth comes from God, and therefore its immediate source (whether in Paul or in Plato) is unimportant, compared with its ultimate source (in God). The truth moreover was to be tested by the truth disclosed in Christ and scripture. (A parallel to this may be seen in his controversy with Luther, in which Luther accused him of giving to reason a role superior to that of the word. Zwingli answered the charge precisely by stating that his appeal was not to reason itself, independent of faith, but to the reason of the believing man, in other words to reason rooted in faith.)

For Zwingli all goodness, like all truth, comes from God. Therefore he took with deep seriousness the instances of good men who were not Christian. In his vision of heaven in *An Exposition of the Faith* Socrates was to be found as well as Samuel, Aristides as well as Abraham. But good pagans like Socrates were not good or in heaven because of something in them apart from God or independently of his work of redemption in Christ. It was not their goodness that put them there;

rather was their goodness evidence that they had been elected by God in Christ before the foundation of the world. Zwingli's placing of particular people in heaven is open to obvious objection, not least in terms of his own theology which allows that we can never know with certainty whether another person is elect. Zwingli's attitude to people (in his case in the past) who were not Christian and to writings which were not dependent on the biblical revelation foreshadows at points some of the modern discussion of the relation of Christianity to other religious faiths and offers some insights for it.

A Theocentric Theology

The stress on the Bible was in itself a part of and a witness to the theocentric character of Zwingli's theology. This found distinctive expression in a vital element in Zwingli's theology and preaching: the attack on idolatry. This corresponds in a measure to Luther's attack on justification by works. Idolatry means a placing of one's trust in the creature and not the creator. Jeremiah asserted this in the words: 'They have forsaken me, the fountain of living water, and have hewn out for themselves cisterns, broken cisterns, that can hold no water' (2: 13).

Zwingli's position was expressed in the fifty-first article in 1523: 'He who gives this authority [to remit sins] to the creature takes away the honour that belongs to God and gives it to one who is not God.' (Z I 464.1–2.) This conviction lay behind his attack on a range of medieval practices and beliefs, such as the intercession of the saints, the use of images, the doing of so-called good works, and a reliance on the sacraments. Zwingli's contrast between faith in God and faith in outward things probably also reflects a negative attitude to outward things which he sees both as leading from God rather than leading to him, and as symbols of what man does rather than of what God does. It is at this point that Zwingli and Luther are in sharpest contrast. Their difference here reflects their different ways of understanding God and creation, and the fact that Zwingli has a Greek as well as a biblical view of the opposition between flesh and spirit.

The theocentric emphasis can be seen also in the sovereignty of God, which shapes the whole of Zwingli's theology. It affects the understanding of God (with a stress on the Spirit and on the divinity rather than the humanity of Christ), of salvation (with a stress on God's providence and election), of church and ministry, and of word and sacrament (with a stress on the inward working of the Spirit rather than the outward means). It is also expressed in his theocratic view of society.

The theocentric emphasis is combined with a strong sense of the opposition of outward and inward, flesh and Spirit, which is part of Zwingli's humanist heritage. (This Greek view exists in Zwingli alongside the biblical opposition of flesh and Spirit, where flesh is the whole person and Spirit is the Holy Spirit.) This combination lies behind Zwingli's view of the sacraments. It separates him from Luther and in a measure from other Reformed theologians, such as Bucer, who combined the two more positively. Of course other influences are also at work here, such as the stress on inwardness in the modern devotion and a reaction against a superstitious regard for externals in much medieval religion.

The opposition of inward and outward was an element in Zwingli's opposition to outward forms in religion. It helps to explain why someone as musical as Zwingli (he played an array of instruments) could banish music and singing from church. Singing could distract from true spiritual worship, just as images inside church could, though not necessarily those outside. In worship as in the whole of life the glory or honour of God was fundamental.

Zwingli's Approach to Reformation

In Zwingli's approach to reformation, teaching and timing were fundamental. He had a strong sense that there was a right moment and a wrong moment for saying or doing something, and in this context he frequently alluded to the danger of casting pearls before swine. His was not the way of the revolutionary—a quick sermon and then out with the hammer and sickle! In his case, let us say, a sermon against idolatry and then out with the hammer to smash the statues and a sickle to slash the pictures. Nor even for him the traditional way of the established church leader, the way of instant legislation, as though changing the church's laws and structures would magically produce reform.

He said of the revolutionaries who wanted to destroy images without more ado, 'Let them first teach their hearers to be upright in the things that pertain to God, and they will immediately see all these objectionable things fall away.' 'Teaching should come first, and the abolition of images follow without disturbance.' (Z III 899.33–5, 906.8–9: *Works* iii. 330, 337.) To misquote Chaucer, he taught and afterwards he wrought. Preaching and persuasion came first, whether by book, or sermon, or public disputation. The persuasion led to pressure from the people for change, and then—at least in many instances—there followed legislation and action. In Zwingli's wise words:

> You can easily persuade an old man to leave his chair if you first put into his hand a staff upon which he can lean, when otherwise he will never listen to you but rather believe that you are trying to entrap him into falling upon the pavement and breaking his head. So the human mind must above all be led to an infallible knowledge of God, and when it has duly attained that, it will easily let go false hopes in created things. (Z III 891.3–8; *Works* iii. 321.)

He advocated that one should first 'restore to their creator the hearts that are given over to this world' before trying to abolish the mass and cast out images (Z V 393.19–22; *Works* ii. 31). He was concerned also about the weak and argued that 'to press on regardless of the weak is the mark not of a strong but of a restless spirit which cannot wait until the poor sheep can catch up behind' (Z IV 255.9–13; LCC xxiv. 158).

With such an approach to reform (at least in outward things), it is not surprising that when changes came they lasted so long. The most notable example is that of organs. They were abolished in 1524 and destroyed in 1527. Apparently Zurich did not have an organ again until over three centuries later in 1848, and even then because of opposition it was not consecrated for five years. Zwingli's church, the Great Minster, did not have one till 1874—350 years after the last one had been played there.

His sense of the right time may express a naturally cautious approach. At several points he held back when others took an initiative. He was present when others broke the Lenten fast in 1522, but he did not break it himself, although he defended those who did. He attacked images before the second disputation in October 1523, but he did not break them as others did, although he afterwards visited in prison those who had done so. He supported marriage for ministers, but although he married early in 1523 he did not make his marriage public until 2 April 1524. He advocated the use of German rather than Latin in worship, but it was Jud who first introduced it, not Zwingli.

A Social Reformer

The Reformation was clearly and fundamentally concerned with people's personal faith in God, but it was also social. In some places it has been fashionable to speak of the Reformation of the sixteenth century as concerned with God and the reformation of the twentieth century as concerned with man. Luther, it is said, wrestled with the question, 'How can I find a gracious God?', whereas we wrestle with the question, 'How can I find a gracious neighbour?' There is a truth in this half-truth, or perhaps a half-truth in this truth. The Reformation of Luther and Zwingli, Bucer and Calvin, was rooted in the discovery of a gracious God. But as there is no fire without heat, so there is no faith without love, no finding a gracious God without becoming a gracious neighbour. For Zwingli as for Luther faith is active in love, but for Zwingli in addition one of the purposes of the law is to show us God's will so that we may live in accordance with it.

Thus the seemingly modern idea that churches or church property should be sold or adapted for the poor is not a new idea. Zwingli, like Bucer, recalled that Ambrose sold chalices to ransom prisoners of war. Furthermore it was natural for Zwingli to tell people to spend their money not on images but on the poor, and to see that monasteries were turned into schools or hospitals or places for the poor. His profoundly biblical (though not literalist) theology enabled him to come afresh to social questions (such as marriage and tyrannicide) and offer new approaches.

A Political Reformer

The Reformation, however, was political as well as social. Zwingli's social concern was not simply ambulance work, helping the poor when they were down to stand up, although he was certainly not concerned with a fundamental change in the structure of society as we understand that today. His aim was to build a Christian society, a society ordering its life according to God's word, in which preacher and prince (or in his case the council) were both servants of God.

The political emphasis can be seen in his patriotism. He was an intense patriot years before he was a reformer, and engaged with political questions from the beginning of his ministry. In particular he opposed the mercenary system—attacking those who made a profit from hiring out their fellow countrymen to foreign powers as well as deploring the lowering of moral standards and the self-indulgence that followed from foreign contact and cheap money. These attacks led to his departure from his first parish in Glarus, but helped his later move to Zurich.

In Zurich he dealt directly with social and political issues in his preaching, and did not hesitate to name names in his sermons. He portrayed the minister in terms of the prophet, and encouraged others to engage in a ministry that was social and political. He did this notably in his sermon on the shepherd or pastor, preached to some 350 ministers at the second disputation in October 1523. He used the example of Elijah and Naboth's vineyard to show that the prophet is obliged to challenge those in authority not just when the whole people suffers but also when only one person suffers injustice. In the light of John the Baptist's challenge to Herod he declared:

From this we learn, that the shepherd must handle and oppose everything which no one else dares to, with no exception, and he must stand before princes, people, and priests, and not allow himself to be frightened by greatness, strength, numbers, nor any means of terror, and at God's command not cease till they are converted ... (Z III 34.3–5, 35.30–36.2.)

A Practical Reformer

There was also a practical element in Zwingli's approach to reformation. Zwingli had no doubt that God's will would prevail, but he stood clearly in the tradition that was to find expression in the famous words ascribed to Cromwell: 'Put your trust in God and keep your powder dry!' One of his most astonishing writings is an actual plan for war, which is well regarded by some military experts. It included detailed instructions about such matters as the disposition of the troops, the time of day or night for attack, and the sort of blasts to be blown on the trumpet. Its concern was not essentially a military one. Its point for Zwingli is clear in its opening words. 'In the name of God! Amen. The author has produced this plan to the honour of God and in the service of the gospel of Christ, so that violence and oppression do not gain control and suppress the fear of God and innocence of life.' (Z III 551.1–5.)

His concern in this was with the preaching of the gospel. That lay behind his *Plan for a Campaign*, as it did with the later battle against the five cantons. In June 1529, when Berne was hesitant about war with them. Zwingli wrote about the necessity to secure the preaching of the gospel. 'This is the end I have in view—the enervation of the oligarchy. Unless this takes place neither the truth of the gospel nor its ministers will be safe among us.' (Z X 147.5–7.)

This practical concern lay behind Zwingli's attempts to forge alliances with other states and cities. Yet in 1531 he would not compromise his view of the eucharist (even so far as to subscribe the Tetrapolitan Confession of Bucer) in order to join the Schmalkald League. Yet the league was formed to defend the preaching of the gospel and its members included allies such as

Strasbourg and Constance and Philip of Hesse. 'The business of the truth is not to be deserted, even to the sacrifice of our lives. For we do not live to this age, nor to the princes, but to the Lord.' (Z XI 340.2–4.)

Besides the practical and often political approach which distinguished him from Luther, there was a practical approach which in some cases was common to them, in particular the recognition that new forms of worship were needed to give expression to the rediscovery and reformulation of the Christian faith. Recent study has shown something of Zwingli's originality here. A reformation lives only as it finds outward forms which embody what it expresses. It is part of the success of Zwingli that he and others gave such forms to the Reformation in Zurich, both in worship and in public life.

A Pastoral Reformer

There was also a pastoral and corporate dimension to the Reformation. Unlike Erasmus whom he much admired, Zwingli had a congregation with all the demands that that made on him. His theology was not formed in a quiet study, but under constant pressure and in response to religious and political problems at home and abroad. In a letter to Haller in 1523 he referred to having been called away ten times in writing it. He mentioned the demands made on him on all sides; yet he told Haller not to spare him if he could be of use, as soon it would be quieter. (Z VIII 140.30–5.) To Vadian in the following year he wrote of the haste in which everything was done as he tried to help people and keep deadlines with the printer, whose eye was on the date of the book fair, adding that he did not have in the house a single copy of a letter. (He was in fact without a secretary.) (Z VIII 166.11–167.6.) A year later he wrote to Vadian of being so busy and suffering so much from headaches that if he did not see his pen go forward, he would hardly know what was happening (Z VIII 314.13–15).

It was under such pressure that Zwingli, the theologian and reformer, worked. But he did not work alone. He had his library; he had the years of careful study both of the Greek New Testament and of the fathers which had preceded his coming to Zurich; he had colleagues such as Jud; and he had a circle of learned friends such as Bucer and Oecolampadius. Ministry was much less isolated from colleagues, and theology less isolated from the life of church and society than it often is today—and what was true for Zwingli in Zurich was equally true for Bucer in Strasbourg and Luther in Wittenberg.

These elements in Zwingli's work as theologian and reformer are not all that could be said about him, though they are characteristic and important. His was a theology that was biblical, yet open to truth wherever it is found. It was centred in God, but in the God who has revealed himself in Christ and who is active through the Spirit. His was a reformation that was educational and practical in method, and personal, social, and political in scope. Both the reformation and the theology sprang from one who was not a solitary, but a partner with others in ministry. His aim in it all can be seen in the last words of *A Commentary*: 'All I have said, I have said to the glory of God, and for the benefit of the commonwealth of Christ and the good of the conscience.' His was a theology and ministry which embraced society as well as the individual, but its source and goal were the glory of God.

Bibliography

THE main bibliographies of Zwingli are G. Finsler, *Zwingli-Bibliographie* (Zurich, 1897) and U. Gäbler, *Huldrych Zwingli im 20. Jahrhundert* (Zurich, 1975). An annual list of works since 1972 is published in *Zwingliana*. An English bibliography, less extensive than Gäbler's, is H. W. Pipkin, *A Zwingli Bibliography* (Pittsburgh, 1972).

Zwingli's Works

Most of Zwingli's works are now available in a modern critical edition in *Huldreich Zwinglis Sämtliche Werke* (Berlin, Leipzig, Zurich, 1905–). For writings not yet published in this edition, the nineteenth-century edition *Huldreich Zwingli's Werke* (Zurich, 1828–42) by M. Schuler and J. Schulthess must be consulted. (These editions are referred to by the letter Z and S, usually followed by a reference to the number of the volume, the page, and the line.) Some material, such as Zwingli's marginal notes, has so far not been published or published only in part.

Zwingli's Works in English

A large number of Zwingli's works are now available in English. Many of them derive from the initiative of S. M. Jackson in the early years of the twentieth century. Four volumes were published then and have since been reprinted, while some unpublished translations have been used in the two-volume edition of Zwingli's writings edited by E. J. Furcha and H. W. Pipkin. (An advantage with this edition is that it gives in the text the page reference of the Latin or German original in the critical edition of Zwingli's works.) Besides these there are several works in volume xxiv of the Library of Christian Classics edited by G. W. Bromiley, *Zwingli and Bullinger* (London, 1953); and two writings at the end of S. M. Jackson, *Huldreich Zwingli* (New York, 1901; repr. 1969). A collection of short extracts illustrating Zwingli's life and thought is available in G. R. Potter, *Huldrych Zwingli* (London, 1978). A translation of the colloquy at Marburg is published in volume 38 of *Luther's Works* edited by M. E. Lehmann: *Word and Sacrament*, iv (Philadelphia, 1971).

Jackson, S. M., *Huldreich Zwingli* (New York, 1901; repr. 1969).
——*The Selected Works of Huldreich Zwingli* (Philadelphia, 1901; repr. Philadelphia, 1972).
——*The Latin Works and the Correspondence of Huldreich Zwingli*, i. *1511–1522* (New York, 1912, repr. as *Ulrich Zwingli Early Writings*, Durham, NC, 1987).
Hinke, W. J., *The Latin Works of Huldreich Zwingli*, ii (Philadelphia 1922; repr. as *Zwingli on Providence and Other Essays*, Durham, NC, 1983).
Heller, C. N., *The Latin Works of Huldreich Zwingli*, iii (Philadelphia, 1929; repr. as *Commentary on True and False Religion*, Durham, NC, 1981).
Bromiley, G. W., *Zwingli and Bullinger* (Library of Christian Classics, 24; London, 1953).
Furcha, E. J., *Selected Writings of Huldrych Zwingli*, i. *The Defense of the Reformed Faith* (Allison Park, Pa., 1985).
Pipkin, H. W., *Selected Writings of Huldrych Zwingli*, ii. *In Search of True Religion: Reformation, Pastoral and Eucharistic Writings* (Allison Park, Pa., 1985).

When these works are quoted, the titles are given as (in the above order): Jackson, *Selected Works, Works* i, *Works* ii, *Works* iii, LCC xxiv, *Writings* i and ii, followed by the page from which the quotation has been made. Occasionally the text has been slightly emended, mostly for consistency in spelling and in the use of capital letters.

Books on Zwingli

Full details of the books and articles on Zwingli are to be found in Gäbler's bibliography and the annual lists in *Zwingliana*. The following is a selection of works in English—first, general discussions of Zwingli's thought and, then, books and articles relevant to the various chapters in this book.

General Studies of Zwingli's Thought

Courvoisier, J., *Zwingli: A Reformed Theologian* (London, 1964).
Furcha, E. J., and Pipkin, H. W., *Prophet Pastor Protestant* (Allison Park, Pa., 1984).
George, T., *Theology of the Reformers* (Nashville, 1988), 108–62.
Hall, B., 'Ulrich Zwingli' in *A History of Christian Doctrine*, ed. H. Cunliffe-Jones with B. Drewery (Edinburgh, 1978), 351–70.
Locher, G. W., *Zwingli's Thought* (Leiden, 1981).

Reardon, B. M. G., *Religious Thought in the Reformation* (London, 1981), 91–117.
Stephens, W. P., *The Theology of Huldrych Zwingli* (Oxford, 1986).

Introduction

Locher, *Zwingli's Thought*, 42–71, 340–83.

1. Zurich and the Confederation

Besides the relevant sections in the biographies of Zwingli referred to in §2 and the general histories of Switzerland:

Oechsli, W., *History of Switzerland 1499–1914* (Cambridge, 1922), 1–68

2. Zwingli's Life and Ministry

The following biographies are concerned primarily with Zwingli's life and reforming work:

Farner, O., *Zwingli the Reformer* (London, 1952).
Gäbler, U., *Huldrych Zwingli* (Edinburgh, 1987).
Jackson, S. M., *Huldreich Zwingli* (New York, 1901; repr. 1969).
Potter, G. R., *Zwingli* (Cambridge, 1976).
Rilliet, J., *Zwingli* (London, 1964).

Other studies of Zwingli's life and work and the context of his thought:

McGrath, A., *The Intellectual Origins of the European Reformation* (Oxford, 1987).
——*Reformation Thought* (Oxford, 1988).
Oberman, S. E., *Masters of the Reformation* (Cambridge, 1981).
Ozment, S. E., *The Reformation in the Cities* (New Haven, 1975).
——*The Age of Reform* (New Haven, 1980), 1–222, 290–339.
Rupp, E. G., 'The Swiss Reformers and the Sects: The Reformation in Zurich, Strassburg, and Geneva', in *The New Cambridge Modern History*, ii. *The Reformation 1521–1559*, ed. G. R. Elton (Cambridge, 1968), 96–119.
Stephens, *The Theology of Huldrych Zwingli*, 5–50.
Walton, R. C., *Zwingli's Theocracy* (Toronto, 1967).
——'Zwingli: Founding Father of the Reformed Churches', in *Leaders of the Reformation*, ed. R. L. DeMolen (London, 1984), 69–98.

Among books and articles on particular aspects of the Reformation in Zurich, the following may be noted:

Birnbaum, N., 'The Zwinglian Reformation in Zurich', *Past and Present*, 15 (1959), 27–47.

Pipkin, H. W., 'The Nature and Development of the Zwinglian Reformation to August 1524', Ph.D. thesis (Hartford Seminary, 1968).

Stayer, J. M., 'Zwingli before Zurich: Humanist Reformer and Papal Partisan', *ARG* 72 (1981), 55–68.

Walton, R. C., 'The Institutionalization of the Reformation at Zurich', *ZWA* 13 (1972), 497–515.

Wandel, L. P. *Always among us: Images of the poor in Zwingli's Zurich* (Cambridge, 1990).

Yoder, J. H., 'The Evolution of the Zwinglian Reformation', *MQR* 43 (1969), 95–122.

Zwingli and Erasmus:

Locher, *Zwingli's Thought*, 233–55.

Zwingli and Luther:

Locher, *Zwingli's Thought*, 142–232.

Rupp, E. G., 'Luther and Zwingli', *Martin Luther Lectures*, i *Luther Today* (Decorah, Ia. 1957), 147–64.

Zwingli and the Anabaptists:

Fast, H., 'The Dependence of the First Anabaptists on Luther, Erasmus, and Zwingli', *MQR* 30 (1956), 104–19.

Horsch, J., 'The Rise and Early History of the Swiss Brethren Church', *MQR* 6 (1932), 169–91, 227–49.

——'The Struggle between Zwingli and the Swiss Brethren in Zurich', *MQR* 7 (1933), 142–61.

——'An Inquiry into the Truth of Accusations of Fanaticism and Crime against the Early Swiss Brethren', *MQR* 8 (1934), 18–31, 73–89.

Klassen, P. J., 'Zwingli and the Zurich Anabaptists', in *Gottesreich und Menschenreich Ernst Staehlin zum 80. Geburtstag* (Basle, 1969), 197–210.

3–7. The Bible; God: The Sovereignty of God; Christ: Salvation in Christ; The Holy Spirit: The Spirit and the Word; Salvation

There are relatively few studies in English of the subjects discussed in

Chapters 3 to 7. For a more detailed examination of the issues raised, see:

Stephens, *The Theology of Huldrych Zwingli*, 51–169.

The Bible:

Courvoisier, *Zwingli: A Reformed Theologian*, 27–37.
Davies, R. E., *The Problem of Authority in the Continental Reformers* (London, 1946), 62–92.

God:

Clarke, J. P., 'Zwingli's Doctrine of the Sovereignty of God', M.Litt. thesis (Bristol, 1974).
Stephens, W. P., 'Huldrych Zwingli: The Swiss Reformer', *SJT* 41 (1988), 27–47.

Predestination:

Locher, *Zwingli's Thought*, 121–41.

Christ:

Courvoisier, *Zwingli: A Reformed Theologian*, 38–47.
Locher, *Zwingli's Thought*, 87–94.

8. Word and Sacrament

Courvoisier, *Zwingli: A Reformed Theologian*, 63–78.
Goeser, R. J., 'Word and Sacrament: A Study of Luther's Views as Developed in the Controversy with Zwingli and Karlstadt', Ph.D. thesis (Yale, 1961), esp. 48–60, 67–82, 141–53, 154–66.
Stephens, *The Theology of Huldrych Zwingli*, 170–93.

9. Baptism

Cottrell, J. W., 'Covenant and Baptism in the Theology of Huldrych Zwingli', Ph.D. thesis (Princeton, 1971).
George, T., 'The Presuppositions of Zwingli's Baptismal Theology', in *Prophet Pastor Protestant*, ed. E. J. Furcha and H. W. Pipkin (Allison Park, Pa., 1984), 71–88.
Stephens, *The Theology of Huldrych Zwingli*, 195–217.

10. The Eucharist

Barclay, A., *The Protestant Doctrine of the Lord's Supper* (Glasgow, 1927), 41–106.

Cadoux, C. J., 'Zwingli', in *Christian Worship*, ed. N. Micklem (Oxford, 1936), 137–53.
Locher, *Zwingli's Thought*, 303–39.
Pipkin, H. W., *Zwingli: The Positive Value of his Eucharistic Writings* (Leeds, 1985).
Richardson, C. C., *Zwingli and Cranmer on the Eucharist* (Evanston, Ill., 1949).
Sasse, H., *This is My Body* (Minneapolis, 1959).
Scott, C. A., 'Zwingli's Doctrine of the Lord's Supper', *Expositor*, 3 (1901), 161–71.
Stephens, *The Theology of Huldrych Zwingli*, 218–59.

11–12. The Church; The State

Courvoisier, *Zwingli: A Reformed Theologian*, 48–62, 79–91.
Hunt, R. N. C., 'Zwingli's Theory of Church and State', *CQR* 112 (1931), 20–36.
Locher, *Zwingli's Thought*, 267–76.
Stephens, *The Theology of Huldrych Zwingli*, 260–310.
Walton, *Zwingli's Theocracy*.
Yoder, 'The Evolution of the Zwinglian Reformation', 95–122.

13. Zwingli: Theologian and Reformer

Locher, *Zwingli's Thought*, 31–41.

On Zwingli and the Arts:

Garside, C., *Zwingli and the Arts* (New Haven, Conn., 1966).

On Zwingli and Calvin:

Locher, *Zwingli's Thought*, 142–232.

Glossary

Alloiosis: A Greek rhetorical term used by Zwingli for the exchange or interchange between the human and divine natures in Christ, or as Zwingli puts it 'where we name the one nature and understand the other, or name what they both are and yet understand only the one' (Z V 926. 1–3). See **Communicatio Idiomatum.**

Anabaptist: The word comes from the Greek *anabaptizein* (to baptize again). It was used by the reformers for those who rebaptized adults who professed faith, although they had been baptized as children. The anabaptists held that what happened to the infants was not baptism, as they were not baptized on the basis of faith.

Catholic: The term is used for Zwingli's conservative opponents, although it is not strictly accurate and is not the word which Zwingli used. He used the word papist for those who gave allegiance to the pope and who held to the unreformed teaching of the medieval church. 'I call all those "papists" who respect all human teaching, statutes and vain behaviour, along with the word of God; indeed, they esteem these higher. For the word of God may say whatever it will, they will nevertheless defend the opinion of the Romish popes and reject the word of God.' (Z II 116.12–16; *Writings* i. 95.)

Chalcedon (Council of): A council of the early church in 451 which, among other things, defined the church's understanding of Christ as one person with two natures, human and divine.

Christology: The teaching about Christ, in particular the integrity and relation of the divine and human natures in Christ.

Communicatio Idiomatum: The Latin term for the sharing of attributes or properties. It was used in the early church for attributing to the human or divine nature what belongs to the other or to the person of Christ. This doctrine was used by Luther to explain and defend his understanding of the presence of Christ in the eucharist. See **Alloiosis.**

Corpus Christi (Feast of): Latin for the body of Christ. The Feast of Corpus Christi commemorates the institution of the eucharist. It was established by Urban IV in 1264 and is celebrated on the Thursday after Trinity Sunday.

Eucharist: One of the terms used for the Lord's Supper which was instituted by Christ at the Last Supper. The word means thanksgiving.

Fathers: Writers in the early church, usually from the end of the New Testament period to the Council of Chalcedon in 451.

Host: The bread in the eucharist after consecration, considered as the sacrifice (Latin *hostia*) of the body of Christ.

Humanism: A diverse movement in the later Middle Ages which is variously defined by scholars. It involved a return to the sources (*ad fontes*). In classical terms this meant the language, literature, and philosophy of Greece and Rome, in Christian terms the Bible and the fathers. Erasmus was the most notable humanist in the Reformation period. His importance for Zwingli and others lay in large part in his editions of the fathers and the Greek New Testament, his Latin translation of the New Testament, and his stress on a rebirth of Christianity (*Christianismus renascens*). He was concerned with the reform of the life of the church. There is an emphasis on Christ and especially, but not only, on his example and teaching. The stress is practical rather than doctrinal. His writings were widely influential, including his emphasis on pacifism.

Marcionite: A view named after Marcion, who was excommunicated about AD 144. He was unorthodox at several points related to his fundamental opposition between the law and the gospel of love and between the flesh and the spirit. The first was expressed, for example, in holding that the God of the Old Testament was different from and inferior to the Father of Jesus, who is a God of love, and in his limited canon of sacred writings (ten epistles of Paul and an expurgated version of Luke's gospel). The second was expressed in a docetic view of Christ. (Docetics held that the humanity and sufferings of Christ only appeared to be real.) Zwingli referred to Luther as Marcionite because in his judgement Luther's view of the eucharist was not compatible with Christ's being a man as we are. For example, a human body cannot be in more than one place at a time.

Mass: One of the terms used for the Lord's Supper.

Nestorianism: A view named after Nestorius of Constantinople. It so stressed the distinctiveness of the two natures in Christ as apparently to affirm two persons (a divine Son and a human son) rather than one person with two natures, human and divine.

Pelagianism: A view named after Pelagius. It stressed the role of human beings and their works in their salvation, leading to the idea of human merit. This view is usually seen in opposition to that of Augustine of Hippo (354–430) who placed the emphasis in salvation on God and his free grace.

Pneumatology: The teaching about the Holy Spirit—from the Greek word *pneuma* (spirit). Some scholars have described Zwingli's emphasis on the Spirit as spiritualist, meaning that it stresses the role of the Spirit in separation from the word (that is, from Christ, the incarnate Word, or the Bible, the written word, or word and sacrament, which are the audible and visible words). Others in response have described the emphasis as pneumatological, meaning that it expresses the biblical teaching about the Holy Spirit, who is the third person of the godhead.

Radicals: A term for reformers who were more radical than Luther and Zwingli, in particular anabaptists and spirituals. The former insisted on the baptism (or, as the name implies, rebaptism) of believers, the latter stressed the role of the Spirit. The term is also used to describe those who cannot strictly be called anabaptists until after the first rebaptisms in January 1525.

Sacrament: The term comes from the Latin word *sacramentum* meaning an oath, such as for example the soldier's oath of allegiance. The Latin word also translates the Greek word *mysterion* (mystery) in the New Testament. The term sacrament was used in a variety of ways in the Middle Ages. Peter Lombard used it of seven rites (baptism, confirmation, eucharist, penance, extreme unction, order, marriage) and this became the accepted use. The reformers held that there were only two sacraments (baptism and eucharist) instituted by Christ, but in the Council of Trent (1545–63) all seven were held by the Roman Catholic Church to be instituted by Christ and necessary for salvation.

Schmalkald League: An alliance for the defence of Protestantism made in Schmalkalden in 1531.

Septuagint: The Greek translation of the Old Testament from the third century BC. There was a tradition (not now accepted) that it was done by seventy-two Jewish translators, hence the word Septuagint from the Latin word *septuaginta* (seventy).

Soteriology: The doctrine of salvation, especially interpretations of the work of Christ focused in the cross.

Speyer, Diet of: The Diet of Speyer in 1529 ended the toleration of Lutherans. It led to the protest of six princes and fourteen cities which gave rise to the word Protestant.

Symbolic View: The view of the sacrament which stresses the distinction between the sign (water, bread, and wine) and what it signifies. According to this view the words 'This is my body' in the eucharist are to be understood as 'This signifies my body'.

Transubstantiation: The view that in the eucharist the substance of the bread and wine is converted into the substance of the body and blood of Christ, while the accidents (the appearance) remain. It is the accidents (such as colour, taste, and quantity) of the bread and wine which our senses perceive. This doctrine was defined as a matter of faith by the Fourth Lateran Council in 1215. The reformers rejected it, but it was affirmed by the Roman Catholic Church in the Council of Trent (1645–63).

Via Antiqua (Old Way)—Via Moderna (Modern Way): These terms refer to two schools of theology in the late Middle Ages. The former is associated with Thomas Aquinas and Duns Scotus and held a realist position in the matter of universals, that is that they are things (*res*) not names (*nomina*). The latter is associated with William of Occam and Gabriel Biel and held a nominalist position in the matter of universals, that is that they are names (*nomina*) not things (*res*).

Vulgate: The Latin translation of the Bible, largely done by Jerome (*c.*342–420).

Short Biographies of Some Principal Figures

Bucer, Martin (1491–1551)

A Dominican, who was profoundly influenced by Luther at the Heidelberg Disputation in 1518. He went to Strasbourg in 1523 and was the leading reformer there until his exile to England in 1548. He was closer to Zwingli than to Luther in the 1520s, but sought to mediate between them in the eucharistic controversy. He took part with Zwingli in the Berne Disputation in 1528 and the Marburg Colloquy in 1529. He was also notable as a mediator in colloquies between Protestants and Catholics and for his personal and theological influence on Calvin.

Bullinger, Heinrich (1504–1575)

His father was a priest in Bremgarten. He studied in Cologne where he was influenced by the writings of Luther and Melanchthon. On his return to Switzerland in 1523 he was a supporter of Zwingli's reformation, taking part in the Berne Disputation in 1528. He succeeded Zwingli in Zurich in December 1531, and ministered there until his death. Through his letters and writings he exercised a wide influence in Europe.

Glarean, Heinrich (1488–1563)

His real name was Loriti, the name Glarean coming from his being a native of Glarus. His letter in July 1510 is the earliest extant letter to Zwingli. It is an expression of their humanist interests. He became a friend of Erasmus in Basle and introduced Zwingli to him. On 4 February 1523 he wrote to congratulate him on the success of the first disputation. Like Erasmus, however, he did not continue his support of Zwingli's work as a reformer. A letter of Zwingli in May 1525 speaks of Glarean's opposition to Zwingli and Oecolampadius.

Philip Melanchthon (1497–1560)

His name was Schwarzerd, but he was given the name Melanchthon by his great uncle, the famous humanist John Reuchlin. He became professor of Greek at Wittenberg in 1518. He was soon influenced by Luther and took the lead in 1521 when Luther was in the Wartburg. He participated in the Marburg Colloquy. He was responsible for the Augsburg Confession in 1530 and also for the Wittenberg Concord in 1536, in which Luther's and Bucer's views on the eucharist were reconciled. He participated in colloquies between Protestants and

Catholics. He later became a centre of controversy among Lutherans because of his stand on the Leipzig Interim in 1548.

Myconius, Oswald (1488–1552)

His name was Geisshüsler, but he was given the name Myconius, apparently by Erasmus, while at Basle. He taught classics in Zurich from 1516 and was the key person in Zwingli's invitation to Zurich in 1518. He left Zurich in 1520, to teach in his native town of Lucerne, returning to Zurich in 1523. In 1532, following the death of Oecolampadius, he became the chief pastor of Basle. He wrote the first biography of Zwingli.

Oecolampadius, John (1482–1531)

His real name was Hussgen or Hausschein. He came to Basle in 1515, where he assisted Erasmus in the publication of his Greek New Testament. He was later influenced by Luther's teaching. In 1522 he returned to Basle. His impact as professor and preacher led to the establishment of the Reformation. He participated in the disputations at Baden in 1526 and Berne in 1528 and in the Marburg Colloquy in 1529. He supported Zwingli's eucharistic teaching, though he differed from him on the relation of church and state.

Pellican, Conrad (1478–1556)

A Franciscan. He was a friend of Zwingli from Zwingli's time in Basle, where he later became Professor of Old Testament. In 1526, at Zwingli's instigation, he succeeded Ceporinus in the prophecy in Zurich. He participated in the translation of the Bible and produced a widely used seven-volume commentary on the Bible.

Rhenanus, Beatus (1485–1547)

A German humanist, he published editions of the classics and the fathers. He lived in Basle from 1511 to 1526, becoming a close friend of Erasmus, and then returned to his native Selestat. He supported the Reformation at first, especially in its criticism of matters such as indulgences, but later changed.

Index of Names and Subjects

Alphabetical Index of Zwingli's Works

The works of Zwingli to which reference is made are given in alphabetical order; for the numbers see the next index.

Index of References to Zwingli's Works

The works are given in the order in which they appear in the two editions of Zwingli's works, with those in the modern edition (Z) first, followed by those in the edition by Schuler and Schulthess (S). The number of each work comes first, followed by the title (in English), the year of publication (as given in Z), and the volume and page reference.

Index of Biblical references